Cambridge Elements

Elements in American Politics
edited by
Frances Lee
University of Maryland

POLICY SUCCESS IN AN AGE OF GRIDLOCK

How the Toxic Substances Control Act Was Finally Reformed

Lawrence S. Rothenberg
University of Rochester

CAMBRIDGE
UNIVERSITY PRESS

CAMBRIDGE
UNIVERSITY PRESS

University Printing House, Cambridge CB2 8BS, United Kingdom

One Liberty Plaza, 20th Floor, New York, NY 10006, USA

477 Williamstown Road, Port Melbourne, VIC 3207, Australia

314–321, 3rd Floor, Plot 3, Splendor Forum, Jasola District Centre, New Delhi – 110025, India

79 Anson Road, #06–04/06, Singapore 079906

Cambridge University Press is part of the University of Cambridge.

It furthers the University's mission by disseminating knowledge in the pursuit of education, learning, and research at the highest international levels of excellence.

www.cambridge.org
Information on this title: www.cambridge.org/9781108464918
DOI: 10.1017/9781108628044

First published 2018

A catalogue record for this publication is available from the British Library.

ISBN 978-1-108-46491-8 (paperback)
ISBN 978-1-108-62804-4 (online)
ISSN 2515-1592 (print)
ISSN 2515-1606 (online)

Cambridge Elements ☰

Policy Success in an Age of Gridlock

Lawrence S. Rothenberg

Abstract: *For a quarter of a century, gridlock and polarization hindered changing environmental policy statutorily. Yet, in mid-2016, the Lautenberg Act strengthened the national regulation of toxics - potentially dangerous chemicals employed in US commerce - while winning support from business as well as environmental interests. What might explain such an unusual occurrence? Has the Trump administration undercut the effects of this new law? Do the factors that produced the Lautenberg Act portend that more progressive enactments are possible in the future? We answer these questions by first showing that the Act was a function of the status quo policy changing due to regulatory efforts abroad and in the states, and due to pressures from citizens and non-governmental organizations on firms and industries. Additionally, the same set of influences that brought business and environmentalists together have impacted implementation, as the Trump administration and its allies have not targeted toxics in "deconstructing the administrative state" in the same manner that they have other programs. While the features generating the Act do not provide a general blueprint for change, they demonstrate that, with greater global trade, the actions of states trying to get around national gridlock, and increasing pressures on firms and industries from groups and citizens operating outside politics as conventionally defined, the legislative and implementation processes we observe for toxics may not be unique.*

Keywords: *gridlock, polarization, environmental policy, Congress, EPA*

ISSNs: *2515-1606 (online), 2515-1592 (print)*

ISBNs: *9781108464918 (PB), 9781108628044 (OC)*

1 Introduction: When the Bough Breaks

> Because we cannot change nature, our only available recourse is to redesign our lawmaking processes and institutions to change political and economic incentives as necessary to promote environmental and climate change lawmaking. The nation must restore Congress to its proper role as the first branch for environmental lawmaking.
>
> Richard Lazarus (2014, p. 34)

> Well, here's the good news. ... For the first time in 20 years, we are updating a national environmental statute. For the first time in our history, we'll actually be able to regulate chemicals effectively. And we're doing it in the same, overwhelmingly bipartisan fashion as happened with those pillars of legislation to protect our air, and our water, and our wildlife – the initiatives where Democrats and Republicans first came together to pass laws more than four decades ago. And that doesn't happen very often these days. So this is a really significant piece of business.
>
> Barack Obama, Signing Statement for
> the Lautenberg Act, June 22, 2016

As this is being written, there is a feeling of impending doom among environmental advocates. A president has been elected who is anathema to environmentalists. His administration is championing draconian employment (25 percent) and budget cuts (31 percent; although in 2018 Congress maintained the agency's funding in nominal dollars) to the Environmental Protection Agency (EPA) and has installed an agency head (Scott Pruitt) who specialized in suing the EPA as Oklahoma's attorney general. At the same time, it is withdrawing the United States from the Paris Climate Accord, and engaging in and condoning a wide variety of administrative actions that are considered outright attacks on the nation's environmental health. At the very least, a great deal of effort is being put into unwinding the overwhelming majority of Barack Obama's environmental endeavors. The new president's choices prompted Fred Krupp, longtime leader of the well-known interest group the Environmental Defense Fund

(EDF), to quip, "Trump's position on environmental protection has been consistent: he wants far less of it" (Krupp 2017, p. 73). The World Resources Institute, a well-regarded, nonpartisan organization, writes more soberly that, while America has a strong tradition of environmental stewardship, "U.S. leaders face mounting pressure to ensure that the [country's] economic growth is compatible with the well-being of people and the planet."[1] And with respect to industrial chemicals, the focus of our analysis, one review (Wilson and Schwarzman 2011, pp. 176–177) concluded, "On [its] trajectory, the United States will face growing health, environmental, and economic problems related to chemical exposures and pollution."[2]

From the perspective of environmentalists, the timing of Trump's ascendance probably could not have been worse. Most notably, it occurred after a quarter of a century of gridlock and frequent frustration over an inability to move systematically at a national level toward ameliorating the environment specifically and addressing societal ills generally. As the introductory quotation by Richard Lazarus, an esteemed environmental law scholar, underscores, the ability to act legislatively by enacting statutes or approving treaties was increasingly restricted by polarization, the ideological distance between the two major political parties. Such polarization, typically measured with respect to each chamber of the U.S. Congress, heightened gridlock in the post-1994 era and inhibited legislative action on the environment and policy concerns more broadly.[3] Polarized legislators and parties found it more and more difficult to muster the levels of support needed for policy change, with opponents of proposals typically finding

---

[1] Downloaded from www.wri.org/our-work/topics/united-states.

[2] Note that the latter assessment was offered before the reforms that we are analyzing were enacted.

[3] We use 1994 as a break point in that it was the election year synonymous with the "Gingrich Revolution" (named after the House Republican leader credited as the mastermind of the successful strategy) that brought conservative Republicans to power in Congress. The results raised polarization even further and thwarted many of President Bill Clinton's efforts in the process.

ways to kill legislative initiatives through vetoes, filibusters, and other strategic actions (for a succinct review, see Barber and McCarty 2015).

In these latter years, instead of employing statutes for dealing with new circumstances and issues, policymakers necessarily relied on alternative means of changing the policy status quo. Rulemaking, the administrative process by which an agency issues new regulations – typically drawing on delegated discretion from often ill-fitting and outdated legislation – and a variety of other non-statutory tools (e.g., Executive Orders) were key. Results were often tortuous, inefficient, and legally suspect (as evidenced by the frequent and lengthy judicial challengers that were the norm). Furthermore, as Trump has helped establish, many of these initiatives, particularly those more recently instituted, are vulnerable to presidential attacks depending on the chief executive's ideology or whim.

Yet, in June 2016, when the election of Donald J. Trump as president seemed an unlikely possibility,[4] Congress broke through the legislative malaise to enact a major new environmental law. Although many had despaired that the legislation would ever reach fruition after a struggle that had encompassed well over a decade, Congress passed and the president signed the Lautenberg Act, reforming the 1976 Toxic Substances Control Act (TSCA).[5] Toxics in this definition include industrial chemicals that are used in US commerce, and not necessarily toxics as poisonous substances. The use of such chemicals is basic to our lifestyle, crucial for the products that we buy and use but with potentially large risks to human health and environmental quality. While worries about

---

[4] In line with conventional wisdom, in late June, well-regarded prognosticator Nate Silver (2016) gave Trump a 20 percent chance of making it to the White House.

[5] Formally, the Frank R. Lautenberg Chemical Safety for the 21st Century Act (public law 114–182; for a legislative history, see U.S. House Committee on Interstate and Foreign Commerce 1976). Although the current law is still an amended TSCA, we refer to the TSCA as the pre-2016 statutory world and the Lautenberg Act as the post-2016.

some chemicals, such as asbestos, have gained much public attention, most are unknown to the general public. The Lautenberg Act made it mandatory for the EPA to evaluate existing chemicals against a risk-based safety standard, with unreasonable risks to be eliminated, and gave the agency considerable ability to demand information about a chemical before approving its use. These features were notably stronger than those in the original TSCA, which had dramatically constricted the agency's information and ability to act. Additionally, deadlines were set and efforts were made to assure funding (see Bergeson 2016).

Hence, the proverbial bough broke. It took forty years after the TSCA's enactment, at least twenty-five years after the policy was deemed broken due to a lack of governmental ability to assess chemicals with proper information and then limit them to the extent deemed appropriate, and more than a decade of trying to enact some rationalizing change that many viewed as impossible. But change did, indeed, come. Now, instead of employing existing chemicals or bringing new chemicals to market with little question, chemical firms such as Dow and DuPont would largely have thrust upon them the burden of proof to produce information and demonstrate the desirability of allowing usage.

Even more notable, the Lautenberg Act was enacted after a quarter of a century of no major environmental laws being passed (the Clean Air Act Amendments of 1990 [CAA] was the previous landmark legislation). As Barack Obama opined in the opening quotation of this Introduction, taken from the Act's signing ceremony on June 22, not only did the legislature (a Republican one at that) come together in a show of seeming bipartisan cooperation but, after years of chemical regulation being ineptly regulated, there was now hope for the future.

1.1 Motivating Questions

Why this seeming breath of fresh air (pardon the environmental pun)? And does the Lautenberg Act's promulgation suggest greater optimism for the future than the gloom-and-doom crowd of environmentalists or policy progressives generally possess? Or was this a unique configuration of circumstances, unlikely to be repeated in the immediate or the mid-term futures? And to what extent were environmentalists' hopes for chemical regulations dashed by the way in which the Trump administration, with its general commitment to the so-called deconstruction of the American state, began to implement the new law? Will the pernicious effects of polarization persist beyond the law's enactment and reduce the probability of achieving the Act's goals?

Answering these questions, and relating them to the broader trends in environmental policy and American politics, are our objectives in this Element. Overall, the answers to these questions can be summarized as offering both bad and good news and, along the way, providing important insights into contemporary policymaking and implementation. On the more negative side, the ability to get the Act through was an amalgamation of uncommon circumstances – the Act does not seem to provide a clear blueprint for further policy rationalization. Having said this, it is possible to imagine other policies where similar forces do come together and again generate a willingness and ability to overcome gridlock even among those who are otherwise at odds politically. Also, and more positively, the very features that brought otherwise disparate interests together and made the Act's passage notable also are somewhat, although by no means completely, protecting it from deconstruction by the Trump administration. However, shielding the implementation of chemical regulation from the other efforts of the new administration to weaken environmental policy is not an easy task. Nonetheless, with caveats, our analysis suggests that if forces come together in a polarized world for change in a manner analogous to what produced the Lautenberg Act, then there is a greater chance of implementation success as well.

To answer these questions requires situating toxics and their regulation within both the contexts of American policy and politics generally and of environmental policy specifically. Although toxic chemicals are not as salient to the public as pollution affecting the air and drinking water, there is nothing *sui generis* about industrial chemicals *qua* pollutants that makes them inherently different. However, there are features of the public and private *politics* of industrial chemical regulation that differentiate them from many other regulatory contexts.

Interestingly, few environmental constituencies were pushing hard for a rationalized policy. If pressures from environmentalists were key, we might have expected changes in air or water statutes before those for industrial chemicals. However, a confluence of external circumstances drove action on toxics reform in a way that has not facilitated action on other environmental issues to date.

More specifically, the TSCA was altered because the world was evolving in a manner making the stasis of national regulation unpalatable to business interests. Desire for change among regulated interests presented an opportunity for a deal with those wanting stricter national regulation. Business interests included not only those in the chemical industry but also downstream consumers of chemicals, be they manufacturers who utilized them as inputs (e.g., automobile producers) or retailers who sold the end products (e.g., Home Depot), who made their feelings well known. Compared to the policy status quo under the original TSCA, business interests were generally willing to allow (1) greater regulatory stringency, by shifting the burden of proof toward the producers; and (2) transparency, by limiting the ability of producers to claim that they would lose out competitively by making information public to government officials, interested groups, and consumers. In exchange, they wanted regulatory certainty (not having to worry about new, unanticipated rules popping up, particularly from the American states) and harmonized (equivalent) policies throughout the country. They wanted to do this such that American regulation conformed to rules in the larger industrialized world, notably in the European Union (EU), to an extent greater than previously (since it is easier to meet the same regulations rather than rules that vary by geographic market).

Additionally, although the full effects of the Trump presidency have not been felt as of this writing, we show that initial actions suggest that the same factors that produced the TSCA's reform have conditioned how toxics regulation has been impacted by the new administration's onslaught on the regulatory system. Toxics regulation has been pushed in a pro-business direction relative to both the initial Obama efforts and those of any likely Democratic successor. This pro-business tilt may inflame conflict over implementation, although there would have been business/environmentalist battles to some extent regardless of who occupied the White House. Yet policies on toxics have not been in the Trump deregulatory rifle's crosshairs because business was a party to the enhanced regulation in the first place. Business and its political allies *do not want* to see implementation of the new regulation undermined. Yet implementation may be collateral damage of other efforts to cripple the EPA and regulation generally. Nonetheless, just as the Lautenberg Act's enactment was a product of a set of circumstances that did not characterize earlier environmental laws, its implementation has been different from the new normal due to the preferences of the vested interests.

Given that an atypical set of circumstances led to the Lautenberg Act's passage and influenced its implementation, the Act does not provide a general blueprint for policy reform or rationalization, contrary to some initial enthusiastic claims. Instead, it will take the same kind of forces – changes to the policy status quo by subnational governments or international political actors, and/or private sector pressures – to push usually opposing sides together in support of change. While this might not be an everyday occurrence, in a world where many firms operate in multinational markets, where American states are disposed to get around national political inertia by acting on their own, and where firms face increasing pressure to be socially responsible, we may see other legislative breakthroughs despite polarization. The right set of conditions makes change possible, but not easy: the events surrounding the Act demonstrate just how tortuous it is to effect change *even* when all the stars might seem to align. More positively, should these forces external to the national government induce new statutes, there will also likely be more than normal support to proceed with implementation rather than to undermine it in the post-legislative stage.

1.2 Plan of Discussion

To show why and how we come to these conclusions, we focus our attention on the evolution of toxics regulation from its very beginning to the present within the context of American environmental and public policy. We rely on primary and secondary sources that cover the relevant issues in great depth. We first discuss why the twenty-first century is an appropriate time for reforming the regulation of toxic chemicals. We then review the multiple impacts of legislative polarization and gridlock on environmental and public policy. After providing background on the TSCA and discussing how chemical regulation became a disappointment that seemingly could not be rectified, we turn to what forces then moved business, political, and environmental interests closer together and, ultimately, induced them to produce new legislation in the Obama administration's waning months. We then discuss how the Obama EPA began implementation, how the rather unexpected rise of Donald Trump impacted the considerable subsequent steps required for the Lautenberg Act to take effect, and how the forces that drove the Act's enactment have also structured what we have witnessed *ex post*. We conclude by discussing what we can learn from the Act about the possibilities for dealing with dysfunctional status quos, initiating progressive change, and providing for effective regulation of industrial chemicals.

2 Why Toxics, Why Now?

Whither TSCA? TSCA's primary statutory provisions remain unchanged after almost four decades. This distinguishes TSCA from the evolving nature of EPA's other major statutes over time. It also raises important questions about whether EPA's chemical program is keeping pace with chemical management trends in the

current global economy. These trends include increasing support
for such concepts as sustainability and environmental stewardship.
(Auer, Kover, Aidala, and Greenwood 2016, p. 14)[6]

To recap, our analysis poses three questions: (1) Why were industrial
chemicals addressed in 2016? (2) What does this legislation generally
say about the possibility for substantive, statutorily grounded policy
change under contemporary polarized conditions? (3) To what extent
have these changes been undermined by a presidential administration seemingly hostile to environmental regulation?

　Here, we take our first steps in answering these questions.
As discussed briefly in the Introduction, it is commonly noted, often
in less than muted tones, that Congress has largely excused itself from
environmental policy and politics, at least from enacting relevant new
statutes. Legislators and congressional committees can be quite ran-
corous and impact appointments and budgets, engage in committee
oversight, and the like. Still, those who care about policy progressivity
or advocate for efficient regulatory instruments have voiced frustration with a lack of statutory action.[7] Environmentalists and those just
wanting better policy have sought paths out of legislative inertia to
clear the environmental logjam (Schoenbrod, Stewart, and Wyman
2012).[8] The pressing question is: when do things get so bad that the
proverbial bough breaks?

---

[6] The four authors are veterans of the EPA program, with relevant policy experience in and out of government, and authored this study as part of the EPA
alumni association (www.epaalumni.com/). Obviously, this piece was written
prior to the Lautenberg Act's passage.

[7] By efficient instruments, we mean policy tools that achieve pollution at the lowest
marginal cost. Typically, this principally involves either using taxes to compensate
for the costs of pollution or markets where one purchases and trades the right to
pollute. The movement toward such instruments, as best epitomized in the United
States by the pollution markets created for carbon dioxide and nitrogen oxides as
part of the 1990 CAA Amendments, occurred after the initial wave of modern
environmental statutes in attempting to produce more efficient policies. Very
much in this spirit, at least pre-Trump, after 1990, presidents from both parties
stridently advocated increased utilization of such markets, to little avail.

[8] Of course, a desire to induce Congress to act is not unique to environmental
policy. For a more general discussion, including a call for constitutional reform

Indeed, the prospect of ending legislative policy paralysis vis-à-vis the environment has appeared no more favorable than for the overall congressional agenda – extremely poor (Binder 2017). Dramatic change would appear to depend principally upon the electorate selecting legislators of a very different ideological ilk in the aggregate than has been the norm in recent decades. For example, as we discuss in more depth in the next section, if the distribution of legislators' preferences more closely mirrored that of the 1970s rather than the 2010s, with Democrats less liberal and Republicans less conservative, there would be less polarization and change would be more likely. Alternatively, we could witness periods of far less gridlock and more dramatic change if the filibuster was eliminated for substantive legislation so that only bare majorities were needed in the Senate as well as the House.[9]

The Lautenberg Act's 2016 passage offers a notable, *prima facie*, surprising exception to environmental deadlock. As we detail shortly, this statute dramatically revamped the regulation of toxic industrial chemicals in the United States by altering a forty-year regime created by the TSCA's 1976 passage. The Act created greater regulatory certainty, especially by (somewhat awkwardly) limiting states' abilities to create additional obligations. It strengthened policy by setting a stricter standard for evaluating chemicals and putting a greater onus on business for showing why the use of chemicals should be permitted. In doing so, it moved policy toward harmonization with other regulations, reducing variance in rules to be followed and obligations to be met both within and outside the United States. It also potentially enhanced the vulnerable reputations of the chemical industry and its downstream partners by making them appear more socially responsible.

As this implies, answering our questions of interest requires investigating the evolution of the circumstances leading up to the

---

so that any presidential proposal becomes law if a majority of each chamber approves, see Howell and Moe (2016).

[9] Even if the Senate was not controlled by the president's party, putting a coalition together could make change easier because the president's party would need to win ten fewer members of the Senate opposition to win a floor vote.

Act. We find that the promulgation of the Lautenberg Act was a function of a confluence of conditions – principally coming to the fore well after the turn of the twenty-first century – where external circumstances' impacts made the status quo dynamic and, thus, any marginal adjustments of policy through administrative management unsustainable. Even though Congress and the president had failed for decades to make legislative headway on these issues and for years there had not even been significant administratively induced policy change (e.g., Goldman 2009),[10] external conditions dramatically altered the status quo and created uncertainty about the future. The relevant actors were very dissatisfied with this rapidly changing status quo and the uncertainties about the future. Further, they could not rely on nonlegislative means at the national level for addressing the situation. Such administrative actions were not efficacious given that the driving forces of change were not at the national political level. As such, these actors became sufficiently motivated to – with great difficulty – overcome their coordination problems and agree on common statutory ground.

Put differently, during the time spanning the TSCA's passage to the Lautenberg Act's enactment, the policy status quo changed, even though there had been no significant legislation regulating toxic chemicals. Political pressures from above and below and even outside of the public political realm relocated the policy status quo, in spite of the lack of legislative action. These changes not only moved policy on a liberal-conservative dimension (how strict the rules were) but also created inefficiencies because business interests found themselves having to show regulatory

---

[10] There were attempts to move the ball administratively. These included pushing the bounds of statutory interpretation and trying to induce voluntary participation by industry, such as through the High Production Volume (commonly known as HPV) Challenge Program, which was designed to make data on large-volume toxics available beyond the extent mandated by the TSCA. However, the impacts of such efforts on the regulation of industrial chemicals via the TSCA were not particularly large and proved no match for the external forces changing the status quo (for a discussion, see Stephenson 2006).

compliance with multiple and differing rules covering chemicals that they made or used. These changes in the world induced business interests, not just chemical companies but also those nearer to the downstream markets, to advocate strengthened regulation (e.g., Lovell 2010). While there were specific disagreements over important details, the general thrust of proposals was compatible with environmental interests (e.g., Plautz 2016).[11] The chemical industry advocated enhanced regulation neither to make the EPA more conciliatory toward the industry nor to otherwise obtain government subsidies nor to limit competition in the tradition of agency capture (e.g., Stigler 1971; for a more recent consideration, see Carpenter and Moss 2013). Instead chemical interests and myriad major downstream users of chemicals or products (e.g., the auto, hardware, and toy industries) accepted greater national regulatory stringency in exchange for a more manageable, certain, and harmonized world, with the added benefit of appearing more socially responsible.[12] Unfortunately, for those clamoring for broader change to environmental regulations or for more progressive policy overall, an analogous convergence of circumstances will not occur everywhere. However, there are any number of issues that may fit the bill and be candidates for polarization-induced legislation similar to the Lautenberg Act.

More specifically, the chemical industry was buffeted by changes to the status quo that were not (or were at most indirectly)

---

[11] As we clarify in what follows, environmental groups were not in complete agreement (and many major environmental organizations – reflecting their traditional focus on media-based [air, water, land] regulation – sat out the process altogether). Nonetheless, overall, environmental groups had a seat at the table and, on net, viewed the new legislation as a substantial step in the progressive direction.

[12] For example, regarding industry costs, it was estimated that the Senate's 2015 TSCA reform proposal would have annual costs to manufacturers, processors, importers, and users of chemical substances in the $150 million range (Congressional Budget Office 2015). While a modest amount, this is only the tip of the compliance iceberg. The estimate covered only direct costs of meeting regulations and not, for instance, the potentially far more substantial expense of waiting to get a new chemical to market or of having a chemical excluded from the market altogether.

a function of national-level choices, be they the actions of legislators, bureaucrats, presidents, or federal justices.[13] Firms found themselves facing compliance with a multiplicity of varying and often changing regulations where certainty and harmonization was a strong preference. Even the benign state of affairs with which corporations had traditionally dealt on the national level in the United States was threatening to come apart (e.g., Silbergeld, Mandrioli, and Cranor 2015).[14] Business interests – the chemical industry and downstream actors – therefore, discovered areas of agreement with progressives and environmentalists in advocating greater regulation that was more in sync with what was going on elsewhere. Agreement was not easy, as the degree of change each side wanted and their contrasting desires for stopping separate state obligations required considerable negotiation and coordination.

Before turning to how the Lautenberg Act was produced, it is important to better understand the nature of the forces buffeting chemical producers and users. We consider each in turn.

2.1 The REACH Program and Its Implications

Undeniably, the most important alteration in the larger world, as suggested by even a casual survey of relevant participants, was the EU's 2006 establishment of the Registration, Evaluation, Authorisation and Restriction of Chemicals (REACH) program. The drafters of the REACH were overtly conscious of being the "non-TSCA" (e.g., Vaughn 2015). As such regulations take many years to implement – indeed, there was an eleven-year implementation process with two opportunities for reassessment – it was recognized

---

[13] As we discuss later, a 1991 federal judicial decision regarding the TSCA's application to asbestos benefited the industrial chemical industry by raising regulatory barriers; here we focus on subsequent activities.

[14] This is because, as we elaborate in what follows, multinational compliance would induce firms both to reveal information that they had previously not turned over to agency regulators and to generate new information that would be transparently available, while a big reason for the EPA's ineffectiveness was the agency's and other interested parties' lack of data.

that the REACH's effects would be slow to be felt but far-reaching. The REACH program (and those in countries mimicking these regulations; see Filipec 2017) created a new set of chemical regulations that were more stringent, more transparent, and more expensive to comply with. As mentioned, chemical companies, which generally operate multinationally (for more on the industry and its geographic breadth, see Tullo 2016),[15] need to provide information that they have typically withheld from American regulators about products. Hence, with the REACH's eventual implementation, American regulators, interest groups, and the public would have access to data that, even if domestic policy was not reformulated, would alter the situation that these firms faced in the United States (e.g., Molander and Cohen 2012; see Environmental Defense Fund 2009 for an early instance where REACH data were exploited).

Given that the REACH regulations were a *fait accompli*, in the quest for greater certainty and conformity, firms desired that the United States harmonize its regulations so that they corresponded more closely to those with which they were, or would soon be, complying abroad (not that they wanted new regulations to go as far in terms of degree of regulation [e.g., Hopkinson 2012]). Environmental interests were generally supportive as the REACH was far more progressive than the TSCA. They were concerned with specific issues ranging from animal testing to, most notably, state preemption (i.e., prohibitions on states issuing their own toxics regulations), which needed to be negotiated with the relevant political interests.

2.2 Blue State Pressures

As the mention of state preemption implies, along with pressure from abroad, there were also stresses from governments below. In response to national-level gridlock, some American states – principally the so-called blue states that lean heavily Democratic

---

[15] And, of course, downstream firms, from Apple to Walmart, also may have multinational markets.

(see Gelman 2009) – had begun imposing additional restrictions on chemicals. With the TSCA neither prohibiting nor constructing obstacles to such actions, corporate interests were increasingly confronting the dilemma of different operating rules depending on geographic locality in the United States, often in very large markets (notably California) that could not be ignored. Not only had the status quo become less appealing, but the future looked ever bleaker.

Hence, a condition of business for agreeing to the TSCA's reform was a significant degree of state preemption in exchange for a stricter national policy. To reiterate, this set up conflict with environmentalists and their political allies, as well as with some conservatives ideologically committed to states' rights. Fights over the role of states became the single most important issue of debate, with a significant amount of preemption required to hold the business coalition together and enough limits to deter blue state Democrats from scuttling reform.

2.3 Attacks on Firm Reputations

Finally, in the background were the pressures on firms from environmental interests – frequently engaging in what Baron (2003) has called "private politics" – to deal with toxics as good corporate citizens (e.g., Walsh and Skjoldal 2011). For the past three to four decades, such private political pressures have been on the rise, and environmental issues have been a key flash point. While this increase has many reasons, the development of technology and now social media has certainly placed business interests very much in the limelight and made them potentially vulnerable. Over time, chemical firms have confronted increasingly negative public opinion, symbolized by accidents such as that in Bhopal, India.[16]

---

[16] Bhopal refers to the December 1984 gas leak of methyl isocyanate gas at a Union Carbide subsidiary's pesticide plant that resulted in what was considered the world's worst industrial disaster, killing several thousand and injuring an estimated half million (for a detailed discussion, see Hull, Kou, and Spar 1996).

The industry's poor image was further reinforced by accruing knowledge and concerns regarding the potential harmful effects of chemicals on human health and the environment generally (e.g., Liroff 2008; Schierow 2009; OECD 2012) and about specific chemicals such as asbestos, bisphenol-A (BPA), mercury, and perfluorooctanoic acid (PFOA) specifically.[17] In the 1980s, chemical firms responded by adopting Responsible Care, an industry self-regulation program,[18] which it continued to strengthen over time. Nonetheless, attacks by disgruntled societal interests continued. These efforts impacted not only the chemical industry but also many other firms that sold or relied on chemicals as inputs, particularly for consumer products (e.g., toys and children's products, hardware, and furniture [notably those using fire retardants] – see, for instance, the efforts of the "Mind the Store" campaign pushing consumers to pressure major retailers).[19]

---

[17] While we assume that the reader knows about the dangers of asbestos for respiratory disease and of mercury for the functioning of the brain and the liver, the issues surrounding BPA and PFOA are probably less well known and deserve brief comment. BPA is a synthetic resin used to make clear, tough plastics that has garnered much publicity because of fears of its consumption, especially by infants. For example, while results are not definitive, there are worries that BPA ingestion can affect the brains, behavior, and prostate glands of infants and young children. By the time of the TSCA's reform, eleven states had passed BPA bans for certain children's food and drink containers (it is still widely used in products such as soda cans), i.e., it represents a prime case of states creating different rules for chemical manufacturers and their downstream clients. PFOA is a synthetic chemical made principally by 3M, and it is most closely associated with DuPont's Teflon and, particularly, with its misuse around the latter's West Virginia plant that led to a notorious class action lawsuit. PFOA is emblematic of many of the environmental problems associated with the TSCA, as 3M brought it to market without providing evidence about its negative health effects. Subsequently, concerns arose that it can lead to a variety of cancers, partly because it stays in the environment and in the human body for a very long time.

[18] Responsible Care originated in Canada in 1984 and was exported to the United States in 1988, a period during which the chemical industry was reeling from declining public confidence, the Bhopal disaster, and other high-profile events. For evaluations of the program, see King and Lennox (2000) and Gamper-Rabindran and Finger (2013).

[19] The campaign's website can be accessed at http://saferchemicals.org/mind-the-store/.

Though most environmental groups did not focus on the TSCA per se, business interests were confronted on industrial chemicals in various ways that did not involve direct political appeals. For instance, there were stockholder initiatives pressuring firms to adopt more progressive stances (for some examples, see Welsh and Passoff 2016) and threatened boycotts (e.g., in 2014, widely reported efforts were undertaken to boycott Apple products given the company's employment of toxic chemicals). Attempts were made to impact companies directly and indirectly by pressuring those in their supply chains.

To the extent that the TSCA's reform would reduce these so-called nonmarket pressures, it would be attractive to corporate interests. Essentially, regulation would provide cover. Indeed, Responsible Care (Responsible Care Advisory Panel 2011) openly endorsed TSCA reform, pointing to citizen pressures on business, as did organizations advocating social responsibility, such as the American Sustainable Business Council and the Investor Environmental Health Network (e.g., Schor 2010).

2.4 Recap: A Changing World

For years, environmentalists had known that the EPA's regulation of industrial chemicals was an abject failure. But until the twenty-first century, these assessments, and the evaluations of policy analysts corroborating them, did not induce any effective effort to rectify the situation.

Only when factors not controlled by the TSCA – heightened regulations by nation-states, aggressive actions principally by progressive US states, and increased societal pressures directly on firms and industries – altered the status quo and reduced certainty about the future did things begin to change. The situation involving toxics was qualitatively changed when the TSCA's benefits to key business players were reduced. Hence, a changing world led chemical companies and down-market firms to come to the national negotiating table and advocate progressive change (although preferring less progressivity, and with far more concern about regulatory certainty, than the usual representatives of environmental causes). Given the difficulty of producing statutory agreements in this polarized age, success took considerable time. With polarization, it is often difficult for political parties to keep their membership in line while coordinating with one another so that ideological differences do not undermine joint goals. Often roadblocks are constructed that derail efforts, for example keeping the proposed action off the legislative calendar or allowing other conflictual issues to be attached to the decision so that they must be voted on as one choice.

Indeed, the process for producing change in national chemical regulation was so lengthy that Senator Lautenberg, unquestionably the principal advocate of toxics reform, did not live to see the bill's passage. Instead, the legislation memorialized the late senator. Consistent prognostications that change was just around the corner went unfulfilled for a number of years, leading to a good deal of despair and considerable hand-wringing. Such was the frustration that John Dingell, the retiring head of the House Energy and Commerce Committee, predicted in 2014: "This is a piece of legislation that has sat around and I think will probably sit around until hell freezes over" (Plautz 2014). While slower and more tortuous than many would have liked, success was ultimately realized.

3 Legislative Polarization and Its Implications for Environmental Policy

Understanding the original TSCA and the Lautenberg Act requires putting each of them, and environmental policy generally, in broader context. Despite the tendency of some to consider environmental policy as *sui generis*, the key features necessary for their understanding are largely generic.

Perhaps the most important elements to appreciate are changes in the extent of polarization and resulting gridlock. While not a prevalent feature in the 1970s, at present Congress remains so polarized that gridlock, by which the legislature is unable to change the status quo via statute, constitutes an extraordinary obstacle for those desiring positive action. This is true whether one's preference is to make policy either more or less progressive (e.g., McCarty, Poole, and Rosenthal 2016).

As such, on the most salient environmental issues of the day, such as those associated with climate change, the principal initiatives have been administrative, rather than statutory. Legislators often attempt to influence outcomes through extra-statutory means (i.e., actions not involving direct legislation pertaining to policy), such as budgetary riders, agency oversight, obstructionist threats, and the like (e.g., on such extra-statutory measures, see, e.g., Smith, Roberts, and Vander Wielen 2015).[20] This led one disheartened scholar to put it (Teter 2013, p. 1160), "the only time Congress can make law [institute policy change] is ... without legislating." In other words, Congress has been unable to steer policy through the conventional process of a bill becoming a law. This neither means that the legislature is uninfluential nor that the executive and agencies can operate in an unfettered fashion constrained only by the courts or the extent of agency discretion (e.g., Chiou and Rothenberg 2017). But it makes rationalizing policies to take advantage of experience, new knowledge, or changing conditions extremely problematic.

3.1 The Growth of Polarization

For those unfamiliar with the relevant data on polarization, Figure 1 displays its evolution in the modern environmental period that started with the EPA's 1970 creation by executive action. This figure displays the difference between the Democratic and

---

[20] For example, at one point there was worry that the TSCA's reform would get caught in the legislative crossfire of budgetary fights over reauthorizing the Land and Water Conservation Fund, a 1965 statute designed for directing offshore oil and gas royalties to improving public recreation and access. Conservatives asserted that the Fund was employed too often to purchase more land for the federal government, with senators holding this opinion blocking the reform act until they got an agreement regarding allocation of the Fund's monies (e.g., LaRoss 2015).

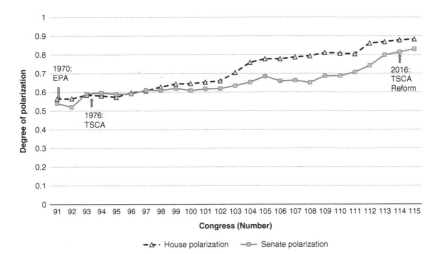

Figure 1 House and Senate polarization – 1969–2016 (91st to 114th Congresses)
Note: Measures the difference between Democratic and Republican Party means by chamber on the first (liberal-conservative) DW-NOMINATE dimension. The 91st and 114th Congresses took place in 1969–1970 and 2015–2016 respectively (we include the first year of the 115th [2017] Congress as well).
Source: http://voteview.com/

Republican Parties' means on the first (liberal-conservative) DW-NOMINATE dimension (a standard measure of ideology on a roughly two-point scale).[21]

The polarization evident in this figure tracks the extent of the problem associated with statutorily altering the environmental status quo. Between 1970 and 1990 (the 91st to 101st Congresses), the

---

[21] Some environmental scholars focus on environment-specific scores of member dispositions, such as those produced by the League of Conservation Voters (LCV), but these ratings correlate highly with general ideology scores such as NOMINATE (for a discussion comparing these issue-specific and general ideology measures, see Anderson 2012). LCV scores and other environmental assessments are best conceptualized as reflecting overall ideological dispositions measured with more error due to the small amount of data incorporated.

period when most national-level environmental lawmaking took place, polarization was much less than in the subsequent period or today. During this earlier period, polarization was rising, especially in the House of Representatives. But Democrats, who tended to be more disposed toward environmental progressivity, always controlled the House during this era. In 1994, the Republicans won control over the Senate and, for the first time since the 1950s, the House. The 1994 Gingrich Revolution constitutes a rough break point, with polarization skyrocketing afterward. As Figure 1 shows, polarization has continued to rise over the past several decades, with the Democrats somewhat stabilizing on the left but the Republicans moving further to the right.[22] By 2016, when the Lautenberg Act was passed, Congress was historically polarized.

3.2 *Implications for Environmental Policy*

Polarization has profound and myriad implications for environmental policy. Indeed, as mentioned, and although there are different perspectives on what constitutes significant legislation, in recent years, it became common to declare that no major environmental statutes passed after the CAA Amendments of 1990. These Amendments, among other things, set up markets for several key pollutants (nitrogen oxides and sulfur dioxide) and represented a bipartisan compromise between the two major parties, enacted under Democratic control of the House and Senate, and Republican President George H. W. Bush (e.g., Bryner 1993). Afterward, Congress became largely a non-player as far as new legislation went (e.g., Lazarus 2015).

This failure to enact new environmental legislation should not be shocking, as it reflects a general trend toward statutory inaction

---

[22] This asymmetry in which Republicans continued to move to the right after Democrats stopping going to the left is somewhat disputed depending on the method used for estimating ideology, although the failure to find this discrepancy is probably an artifact due to specific measurement choices of other scholars (e.g., Tausanovitch and Warshaw 2016). Regardless, there is a scholarly consensus regarding increasing polarization between the parties.

attributable to polarization. For example, examining polarization from 1947 to 2013, McCarty found that in the least polarized term there was 111 percent more legislation relative to the most polarized term (reported in McCarty, Poole, and Rosenthal 2016; but see Grossman 2014).[23] With higher polarization, gridlock prevails, as preferences are too divergent and the ability to produce bipartisan cooperation is extremely modest. Environmental policy is just one of many examples of the resulting stasis.

There are many nuances in understanding the ramifications of no new legislation (for a review of some of the effects of polarization on governance generally, see Lee 2015). Even those opposing government-initiated environmental progressivity recognize the often costly implications of this statutory sclerosis. The ramifications of statutory inertia are profound and frequently negative, regardless of one's ideological perspective. Rather than causing agencies to do nothing, as opponents of additional environmental actions might prefer, policy stalemate may instead operate in alternative and often problematic ways.[24]

While not an exhaustive list, consider three, related, policy consequences associated with gridlocked politics:

1. **Old statutes are applied to new problems for which they may be inappropriate.** Inability to generate new statutes induces agencies to apply extant authorities to different concerns from those they were intended to address (e.g., Freeman and Spence 2014; Deacon 2016). The most obvious such instance in recent years involves climate change, which is principally being addressed administratively by employing features of the CAA for problems for which they were never envisioned.

---

[23] See also Binder's (2017) work on the relationship between gridlock, polarization, and the legislative agenda, which also indicates that polarization leads to more stalemate.

[24] This same logic applies to the actions of the Trump administration, although obviously many of the impacts on the environment per se are negative, trying to rein back the efforts of government. As such, the role of the EPA has often been not to push progressive boundaries but to see to what extent it can limit actions that might be legally required.

(Admittedly, in *Massachusetts* v. *EPA* [549 US 497, 2007], the Supreme Court ruled that the law should be applied to greenhouse gases if they were deemed air pollutants through an endangerment finding.) Given what straightforward interpretations of the CAA would seem to imply, this has meant that the EPA has needed to offer awkward justifications. For example, in contrast to what the CAA would seem to indicate but reflecting what seemed to be sensible regulation, the EPA created rules excluding relatively small greenhouse gas producers from its regulations and including those not falling under the CAA for other pollutants. However, the Supreme Court rejected such efforts (see *Utility Air Regulatory Group* v. *EPA* [134 S. Ct. 2427, 2014]).[25]

2. **Without the ability to amend existing statutes, or to author new legislation, problematic features of old statutes fester.** A host of aspects of existing programs that are statutorily dictated would constitute prime candidates for change under different conditions because they have proven extremely costly relative to benefits or completely ineffective. But an inability to amend or author new legislation *de novo* dictates that these troubles continue. Among other problems not addressed, the Superfund's funding situation is still archaic, made worse by the sunsetting of its original taxing authority, contributing to the EPA's failure to complete its assigned tasks more than thirty-five years after its promulgation. (As this is written, more than 1,300 sites await remediation.)[26] The Endangered Species Act remains an antiquated approach to preservation that those on both the left and the right decry to varying degrees (e.g., see the

---

[25] The Court, while generally accepting the EPA's regulations on stationary greenhouse gas sources, disputed elements of its "tailoring rule" differentiating who was covered (for a discussion, see Freeman 2015). Specifically, the EPA tried to come up with reasoning for why it could ignore the Act's numerical thresholds of 100 or 250 tons of a pollutant per year (as this would be a tough trigger for greenhouse gasses), which the Court set aside given that it unambiguously conflicted with the expressed intent of Congress.

[26] For a thorough review, see Judy and Probst 2009; for a recent discussion, see Environmental Protection Agency 2017.

collection in Adler 2011; for a proposal oriented toward better designing incentives for species preservation, see Boyd and Epanchin-Niell 2017). The ability to deal with nonpoint sources of water pollution remains extremely limited despite the recognition that they constitute our principal source of water pollution and that existing legislation deals with them poorly (e.g., Rissman and Carpenter 2015).[27] The employment of market mechanisms for aspects of air pollution for which they would seemingly be appropriate, cost-effective, instrument choices is prevented (symbolized by the failed legislative proposal for cap-and-trade during Obama's first two years; see, e.g., Frankel 2014).

3. **The courts confront the problematic situation of interpreting agency actions under claims of discretion utilizing old statutes that are seemingly obsolete.** Given the inability of the other branches to produce new legislation potentially places the judiciary in a more influential role. The courts are put in the situation, often in the context of interpreting appropriate agency discretion, of determining how to interpret bureaucratic actions that are claimed to be consistent with seemingly obsolete legislation (e.g., Freeman and Spence 2014). Probably no recent controversy better illustrates this issue than the efforts of the Obama EPA to define, some would say to expand greatly, its authority through interpreting what constitutes navigable waters.[28] While such authority rests with the original Clean

---

[27] Nonpoint water pollution involves water runoff that picks up natural and human-made pollutants and deposits them in bodies of water or groundwater. This contrasts with point source pollution, where pollutants are coming from a fixed point, such as a pipe.

[28] The Clean Water Act of 1972 incorporated the idea of navigable waters, which are linked to interstate commerce, to justify regulation over water bodies whose control might have been seen to rest with the states. Donald Trump derided the attempt to expand the interpretation of navigable as constituting "one of the worst examples of federal regulation, and it has truly run amok" (www.whitehouse.gov/the-press-office/2017/02/28/remarks-president-trump -signing-waters-united-states-wotus-executive). As of this writing, the rule is in judicial limbo while, at the same time, the Trump administration is working toward rescission.

Water Act, the joint attempts of the EPA and the Army Corps of Engineers to broaden the interpretation of such waters has presented a considerable burden to the courts (e.g., Rabkin 2013). New legislation clearly and unambiguously defining navigable waters is an obvious solution – but this is not happening in the present context. Thus, it is not surprising that scholars such as Greve and Parrish (2015, p. 545) argue that "what is needed is . . . a set of [legal] doctrines that give Congress incentives to legislate."

To reiterate, there may be situations where political actors outside of Congress ameliorate the problems associated with polarization and gridlock to a degree. There is *policy drift*, although often in contorted and expensive ways that frustrate environmentalists and drive opponents to distraction (on the notion of policy drift see, e.g., Hacker 2004; for a related discussion with respect to environmental policy specifically in terms of green drift, see Klyza and Sousa 2013).[29]

However, sometimes such discretionary adaptation is insufficient. The status quo can change to such an undesirable degree, and the extent of discretion may be sufficiently limited given what is needed to adjust to changing circumstances, that polarization's and gridlock's pernicious effects might prove unbearable. Put differently, the costs of gridlock may be so great that, indeed, a point is reached where the bough breaks. Statutes may finally get changed in such extraordinary situations not *despite polarization and its consequences but, in a sense, because of them.* The status quo

---

[29] Callander and Krehbiel (2014) posit a formal model of status quo drift in the presence of gridlock and delegation that captures the idea of such administrative impacts. Their model provides conditions under which the delegation of bureaucratic authority may help mitigate some of the negative impacts of policy drift caused by exogenous forces in the political environment that cannot be dealt with by a deadlocked legislature. For example, the EPA has employed its discretion to build more flexibility into the implementation of age-old statutes; one instance is that, in conjunction with the National Highway Traffic Safety Administration, it incorporated the ability of car manufacturers to trade credits in trying to meet heightened Corporate Average Fuel Efficiency standards promulgated in recent years.

becomes so unacceptable that the requisite legislative superma-jority (its size depending on whether or not the president approves of the proposed change) takes on the arduous tasks needed to break gridlock. Toxic chemical regulation in the United States constitutes such an occurrence.[30]

3.3 Putting Policy in Context

Our discussion in this section has laid out the role that polarization and gridlock play in policy generally and in environmental policy specifically. Overall, we expect much more statutory initiative when polarization is low and, conversely, other forces have greater impor-tance in moving policy when polarization is high. We have, however, left the door ajar in that there may be circumstances where the resulting situation gets so bad that polarization, in a sense, induces action. We turn our attention in the next several sections to detailing how the regulation of industrial chemicals fits this mold – both statutory action when polarization is low and the possibility that the situation gets so bad that statutory inertia can be overcome.

4 The TSCA: From Hopeful Beginnings to Universal Failure

> I have signed S. 3149, the Toxic Substances Control Act. I believe this legislation may be one of the most important pieces of environmen-tal legislation that has been enacted by the Congress. . . . In addition,

---

[30] Somewhat in the same spirit, Callander and Martin (2017) formulate a theoretical model where policy decay might induce policy action, leading the legislature generally and the agenda setter specifically to break the gridlock. While their analysis focuses on quality as a second dimension and on expertise, our empirical study is somewhat different – the key issues do not involve expertise per se and the process by which change creates a harmful status quo does not match completely with their notion of quality. In the case of the TSCA's reform, the status quo on what Callander and Martin would character-ize as the first dimension changes. Yet their heuristic, that the world can evolve so that gridlock can be broken with time, is not inconsistent with what we maintain has given forth the Lautenberg Act.

I am certain that the Environmental Protection Agency realizes that it must carefully exercise its discretionary authority so as to minimize the regulatory burden consistent with the effective protection of the health and environment.

> Gerald Ford, Signing Statement for Toxic
> Substances Control Act, October 12, 1976

When TSCA was passed in 1976, there were great expectations that it would improve our understanding of chemical risks and address these risks in a comprehensive multimedia framework. But, for a variety of reasons, TSCA has not been able to fully live up to these expectations.

> Written Testimony of Former EPA Administrator
> Lynn R. Goldman (2015) to U.S. Senate Environment
> and Public Works Committee

As implied in the previous section, the TSCA's passage constitutes, in some sense, the flip side of gridlock and polarization. After an unsuccessful effort to produce a law in 1974, the regulation of industrial chemicals remained on the legislative agenda. There was low polarization between legislators and their parties and a large post-Watergate Democratic majority in both legislative chambers.[31] President Gerald Ford was relatively moderate ideologically.[32] He also was facing a nontraditional election bid given that he had been appointed vice president and then became president after Richard Nixon's scandal-induced resignation. To curry electoral favor, he wanted to establish some environmental *bona fides* but did not want to go too far, either (as his cautionary comments about the EPA reproduced earlier and reports of his unhappiness with the bill

[31] At the time of the TSCA's passage, the Democrats possessed sixty-one Senate seats, and a massive 147 House seat advantage (291–144). Given that the filibuster rules had changed in 1975 to reduce the number of votes needed to sixty, the Democrats had enough votes, conditional on complete party unity, to overcome a Republican filibuster.

[32] Of post-World War II Republican presidents, only Dwight Eisenhower was more moderate than Gerald Ford, who was slightly more moderate than Richard Nixon per standard ideology measures (McCarty, Poole, and Rosenthal 2016).

produced by the congressional conference committee make clear; on the latter, see Russell 1976a).[33] Out of this set of circumstances, the TSCA was enacted. Despite his trepidations, Ford signed the law on October 11 and issued his signing statement on October 12, three weeks before voters headed to the polls.

Put differently, the TSCA passed in a world where polarization and gridlock were modest and circumstances were otherwise favorable. While industrial toxics had not traditionally been at the top of environmental priorities, other major environmental worries had been dealt with in the post-EPA era and concerns involving such chemicals had heightened to some extent. Most notably, there was awareness about contamination of waterways such as the Hudson River by polychlorinated biphenyls (PCBs), which was explicitly dealt with in Section 1 of the enacted TSCA.[34] Hence, toxics became the last of the major pollutants targeted in the initial

---

[33] A review of papers available through the Gerald Ford Presidential Library shows that, for largely electoral reasons (voters would approve of actions mitigating harmful chemicals), the administration favored a toxics bill if it would not prove too much of a burden for the chemical industry or embolden the EPA too much. With respect to the administration's concerns, for example, it was leery of premarket screening requiring new chemicals to be evaluated with considerable data before they came to market and any enlargement of EPA budgets to facilitate aggressive enforcement (Duval 1975). Emblematic of the Ford administration's electoral viewpoint was the private advice proffered to Chief of Staff Dick Cheney by A. James Reichley (1976, p. 14), who was serving as a consultant for the 1976 election:

We should make more of the ongoing environmental activity being carried on by the Administration. I am told that the environmentalists' current top priorities are: amendments to the Clean Air Act; the toxic substances control bill; and strip mine regulation. I am not familiar with the policy issues involved, but wherever we can responsibly lean toward them, it would be politically helpful.

[34] PCBs are combinations of carbon, chlorine, and hydrogen, and were widely used in electrical equipment from the chemical's original production in 1929 until 1977. Human exposure, such as through consuming fish, has been associated with a variety of maladies and possible damage to the reproductive system. The aftereffects of PCB usage, such as those ensuing from dumping in the Hudson River by General Electric (resulting in the largest environmental dredging project in American history from 2009 to 2015), were receiving a great deal of public attention and were widely discussed in conjunction with the TSCA's creation (e.g., Russell 1976b; Flippen 2006).

wave of regulation passed in the era immediately after the EPA's 1970 creation.

4.1 Reasons Given for the TSCA's Passage

Explanations for the TSCA's passage not only provide insight into why the statute became law but also foreshadow the policy's subsequent problems and the reasons they were not dealt with effectively. Specifically, standard discussions of the TSCA's enactment emphasize four factors:

1. Increasing elite worries about the effect of toxics on the environment (e.g., see especially the Council on Environmental Quality's [1971] white paper on toxics which, in many respects, provided the foundation for the legislation);
2. A desire to fill gaps not covered by media-based statutes (i.e., laws focusing on air, water, or land) passed in the previous half-dozen years (e.g., dealing with the transfer of pollutants from one media to another; see Humphreys 1976);
3. Efforts to make an initial foray into pollution's prevention rather than its *ex post* treatment (e.g., Markell 2010); and
4. A need to generate new information not required by previous legislation about the effects of toxics (e.g., Applegate 2008).[35]

In enacting the TSCA, Congress essentially delegated the EPA authority over all industrial chemicals. While the legislation contained many sections (for detailed overviews, see Schierow 2009, 2013), among its most important features were that the EPA was to:

- Require manufacturers and processors to conduct tests for existing chemicals (roughly 55,000 to 60,000 at the time of passage –

---

[35] According to many, such as the EPA's head at the time of enactment, Russell Train (e.g., Interview with Russell Train by Don Nicoll 1999), J. Clarence (Terry) Davies, who was at the Council and then moved to the EPA, was the TSCA's principal architect. His blueprint was then amended as it wound its way through the legislative process (for an insightful oral history by Davies, see The Toxic Substances Control Act: From the Perspective of J. Clarence Davies 2010).

estimated at about 80,000 to 85,000 today) if there is an unreasonable risk of injury to health or the environment, or the chemical is produced in very large volume and there is a potential for a substantial quantity to be released into the environment, or there is a risk of substantial or significant human exposure;

- Require manufacturers, importers, and processors to notify the EPA at least ninety days prior to producing or introducing a new chemical (a premanufacture notice), and provide any useful information in evaluating the chemical to the EPA;
- Issue the least burdensome (a key term) regulations possible; and
- Provide broad protection of confidential business information (CBI) furnished to it.[36]

Clearly, there was an attempt to balance the environment with business costs and protections, as well as the delegation to the EPA of a rather broad mandate in terms of what was reasonable versus unreasonable. How this played out was not particularly favorable to environmental interests.

4.2 The TSCA's Aftermath

Much more was expected from the TSCA than was realized. Several basic, related, features of the bill, each stemming from Congress's rejection of key components of the 1971 Council on Environmental Quality recommendations would appear to explain this lack of impact. Congress's seeming attempt to balance the protection of the environment with the wishes of the chemical industry, the latter being a key component of the economy (Applegate 2008), proved particularly problematic for the efficacy of the eventual bill (The Toxic Substances Control Act: From the Perspective of J. Clarence Davies 2010).[37]

---

[36] For more detail, see www.epa.gov/tsca-cbi.
[37] Davies particularly points the finger of blame at the Department of Commerce for a great many of the dysfunctional aspects of the enacted legislation.

One result was that the EPA was ill positioned to generate the relevant information needed for evaluating chemicals, be they existing or new (although new chemicals were to be regulated more vigorously), despite the recognition that such data were essential. Hence, the chemical industry was not incentivized to step in and provide the agency with needed data. Unlike pesticide producers, for example, chemical manufacturers were *not* required to produce such data to sell their products, so ignorance was truly bliss.[38] The firms' disincentives to generate information that could be potentially employed by the EPA in a manner injuring them created a "data trap" (e.g., Vogel and Roberts 2011; see also The Toxic Substances Control Act: From the Perspective of Charles M. Auer 2010). In other words, the EPA was placed in a position that made meeting its purported objectives impossible. For example, many condemnations of DuPont concerning the firm's keeping Teflon's negative effects quiet were linked to the weakness of the EPA's informational position under the TSCA and the company's concomitant choice to hide behind the cloak of CBI (e.g., Lerner 2016).

Another vexing element of the eventual statute was, as foreshadowed, that the TSCA's requirement to demonstrate unreasonable risk was a quintessentially ambiguous term. *Ex ante*, defining unreasonable risk necessitated considerable clarification at the agency or judicial level. Whatever definition was adopted, the data trap made establishing that a chemical satisfied it extremely challenging.

This difficulty was underscored by the 1991 appellate court ruling in *Corrosion Proof Fittings et al.* v. *EPA* (947 F.2d 1201 (5th Cir.)) (heretofore *Corrosion Proof Fittings*; see Applegate, Laitos, Gaba, and Sachs 2011 for a detailed discussion). This decision stopped

---

[38] Pesticides are regulated under the Federal Insecticide, Fungicide and Rodenticide Act (FIFRA), which, although originally passed in 1910, was updated as part of the wave of modern environmental regulations in 1972. After that point, the manufacturer bore the burden of proof to show that the pesticide merited registration by being consistent with human health and protection of the environment.

the EPA's considerable and costly efforts to restrict asbestos in their tracks. (Interestingly, while most people the author confronts in casual conversation believe that asbestos is illegal, it is not as of this writing.) In its ruling, the court interpreted the TSCA's criterion that restrictions be the least burdensome as requiring that *the more severe the limit, the greater the data needs*. Thus, even for asbestos, the agency was judged to lack the requisite evidence documenting sufficient risk relative to what was proposed.

As such, the 1991 *Corrosion Proof Fittings* decision constituted the break point where the TSCA was proven clearly unworkable, as even this widely feared and extraordinarily harmful chemical could not be banned. Although litigation and fears of harmful health and environmental effects have substantially reduced its usage, in the present day asbestos continues to be imported from places such as Brazil, China, and Russia (domestic production came to a halt by the early twenty-first century) for specialized uses for which there are no clear substitutes.[39] Strikingly, with Canada announcing a 2018 ban, the United States will be the final advanced industrial nation (out of fifty-five) to ban the substance even if it does so under the Lautenberg Act.

4.3   Reasons for Failure

The quote from Goldman's testimony at the beginning of this section is just one of many that we could provide that reflects the consensus viewpoint that the TSCA was not particularly successful. Consistent with the failure to adopt some of the Council of Environmental Quality recommendations, one explanation given for the TSCA's disappointing results is that elements of the legislation were badly written (e.g., Everts 2012). As should be clear, such assessments should be unsurprising given that the TSCA was

---

[39] An example, and the principal use of raw asbestos in the United States, involves the chlor-alkali industry, which employs "semipermeable asbestos diaphragms" to separate chlorine, caustic soda, and hydrogen. Currently, forty-four large chlorine production facilities utilize asbestos for this purpose (Walsh 2017).

a compromise between competing interests, not to mention that it dealt with a complicated set of issues for which not all outcomes could have been anticipated. In terms of poorly drafted legislation, as discussed, the most immediate culprits were the provisions producing a lack of information on chemicals but requiring a high standard for unreasonable risk. By extension, soon after this poor construction was absolutely clear with the *Corrosion Proof Fittings* decision, there was too much legislative dysfunction – not to mention chemical industry opposition juxtaposed against environmental interest group ennui – to do anything substantial to remedy the situation.[40] Ironically, the worries internal to the Ford administration when the statute was enacted, such as the high costs on business of premarket notification for new chemicals, proved largely unfounded.

At a broader level, additional, interrelated reasons were offered for the TSCA's disappointing returns. Several were consistent with the TSCA being last in line chronologically, filling gaps in existing policy (e.g., Markell 2010), such that toxics was characterized as an orphan policy. Industrial chemicals, whether they ended up in air, land, or water, were being dealt with by an agency principally designed to regulate by media. Also, no dedicated revenue stream existed to pay for the agency's incurred costs (e.g., Everts 2012). Consequently, the TSCA was considered the law of last resort, when others were inapplicable to a problem.[41]

In a related vein, and perhaps unsurprising given that constituents tend to care principally about air and water pollution rather

[40] On interest group disinterest, Victor Kimm, who was a key EPA policymaker at the time, lamented that "there wasn't any public interest group or environmental group pressing [for vigorous implementation]" (The Toxic Substances Control Act: From the Perspective of Victor J. Kimm 2011, p. 15). Similarly, the policy was given little popular attention: the Vanderbilt Television News archive, which categorizes what the national news has covered, shows not a single story about TSCA implementation when one searches for stories on the TSCA (there were two stories about the legislation's enactment).

[41] See the oral history of the director of the Office of Toxic Substances, Glenn Schweitzer, when the TSCA was passed (The Toxic Substances Control Act: From the Perspective of Glenn E. Schweitzer 2010).

than something less immediate like industrial chemicals, legislators who might have pushed for effective implementation took little interest in doing so (and the few who were in the Congress at the time of the legislation's passage quickly left). This was reflected in few oversight hearings being held and, in those that were, complaints about the policy falling between the cracks (e.g., U.S. Senate Committee on Energy and Public Works 1994, which became known as the Reid hearings). In fact, the Senate's Energy and Public Works Committee, while responsible for toxics, was not even involved in the TSCA's writing and was considered to lack expertise and interest at best (Everts 2012).[42]

Similarly, and as implied earlier, and again perhaps not surprising given what constituents and contributors care most about, there were few environmental interest groups consistently taking up the cause of industrial toxics (in the years before the Lautenberg Act, the EDF became the rare group prioritizing change; for an example of the group's well-developed perspective, see Denison 2009). Conversely, the chemical industry was mobilized and supportive of what became the status quo (this was a factor in why the procedural deck [the set of rules defined for the policy's implementation] in the TSCA was stacked so much in favor of chemical interests; see, e.g., McCubbins, Noll, and Weingast 1987).[43]

---

[42] For example, Steven D. Jellinek, who was the first assistant administrator for toxic substances at the U.S. Environmental Protection Agency, and then the assistant administrator for pesticides and toxic substances, describes the situation in the following manner:

So, here you have a new law that people have very high expectations for, and unlike most laws, it had no advocate or sponsor in the Congress. The guys in Environment and Public Works made sure EPA did – or they tried to make sure EPA did – what they had intended when it came to Clean Water, Clean Air. They were very much involved, pushing the agency on the policy, and on implementation. When it came to TSCA, the Senate guys could care less. They just kind of ignored it, because they hated it (The Toxic Substances Control Act: From the Perspective of Steven D. Jellinek 2010, p. 6).

[43] For example, as veteran policymaker James Aidala put it, "The non-profits ignored TSCA. That's been part of the problem" (The Toxic Substances Control Act: From the Perspective of James V. Aidala 2010, p. 40).

Also, along the same lines, the EPA was notably not aggressive under Ronald Reagan's administration (1981–1989) in implementing policy. Even Reagan's director of the EPA's Office of Toxic Substances notes that he was "frustrated we weren't sued"[44] by environmental interests to jump-start the process – so there was no hope that administrative creativity would help even after the Bhopal disaster. Unlike other politically salient environmental areas where Democratic majorities in Congress wrote statutes to move policy in more progressive directions in response to Reagan's efforts, there was inaction on industrial chemicals.

Thus, it was not surprising that it would take fifteen years after the TSCA's initial enactment and the 1991 *Corrosion Proof Fittings* decision, when it became clear that the program required an unattainable level of data and analysis given its other provisions, for the full extent of the TSCA's problems to be recognized. After *Corrosion Proof Fittings*, calls came for statutory change, including from the EPA (for a review, see Bergeson, Campbell, and Rothenberg 2000). While statutory tweaks would seem a natural thing in any complex situation where there is learning and updating and the state of the world is changing (e.g., new types of chemicals being created and new understandings of how chemicals impact human health and the ecosystem being developed), conditions were exceptionably unfavorable. Constituencies for reform were weak, the chemical industry was not unhappy with the statutory status quo, and polarization and corresponding gridlock were soon defining Washington. Ironically at the EPA's request, the 1994 Reid hearings were held and others, such as the Government Accounting Office (1994), advocated statutory change. But, ironically, such actions occurred right before the Republican landslide victories in that year's mid-term elections and the corresponding explosion of polarization. What little momentum for reform that had existed was wiped out.

---

[44] See The Toxic Substances Control Act: From the Perspective of Don R. Clay 2010, p. 7. For an even more vigorous discussion by an important insider of the Reagan administration's impact, see Aidala's comments (The Toxic Substances Control Act: From the Perspective of James V. Aidala 2010).

Instead, analogous to many other policy areas characterized by policy drift, the EPA tried to adjust the status quo somewhat via its discretionary authority. It employed various administrative means, including voluntary programs and stretching interpretations (e.g., of what constituted significant new uses of chemicals as a means of regulating existing chemicals or what information could be released to the public). These jerry-rigged administrative attempts to right the ship proved Band-Aids at best, and the TSCA continued to be widely deemed as ineffectual and, consequently, derided (e.g., Adelman 2010). There appeared little hope for the future throughout the last term and a half of the Clinton administration and much of the George W. Bush presidency.

4.4   The TSCA – Government Failure

In short, the TSCA seemed a classic example of government failure (e.g., Orbach 2013). While few would dispute a potential role for government for dealing with the externalities created by using industrial chemicals on human health and the environment (i.e., the harms that were not factored into the price paid by the user), the choices made by legislators, the EPA itself, and the courts left an ineffectual policy in its wake. The inability of elected political officials to rectify this situation meant that the gaps that the TSCA was supposed to fill remained glaringly open.

5   The New Millennium: What Changed?

> Our nation's main statute governing chemicals policy – the **Toxic Substances Control Act (TSCA)** – is seriously flawed and needs fundamental reform.
>
> EDF (April 2016)[45]

---

[45] Downloaded from www.edf.org/health/policy/chemicals-policy-reform. Bold in original.

ACA [American Coatings Association] supports a modernized, federal chemicals management program that will not only improve the public's confidence on the safety of chemicals, but will also provide businesses with much-needed certainty and consistency in the marketplace.

American Coatings Association (April 2016)[46]

Thus, circa 1995, few were predicting TSCA reform. The policy had never been of much interest to legislators, voters, or most environmental groups. And, indeed, for a very long time, the law's implementation was routinely condemned by those outside the industry who cared. For example, only roughly 200 of 85,000 chemicals were ever tested and voluntary programs and administrative palliatives were clearly inadequate. Yet calls for change fell on deaf statutory ears. Such indifference existed despite much being learned about the possible negative impacts of industrial chemicals and about what can determine such effects given time and duration of chemical exposure (e.g., Silbergeld, Mandrioli, and Cranor 2015). Nor did the emergence of new concerns, such as those related to nanotechnology (for a discussion of the regulation of chemicals related to nanotechnology, see Hanshaw 2015)[47] and synthetic biology (e.g., worries about genetically modified organisms) being recognized (e.g., Schierow 2009), lead decision makers to move on reform. Even the emergence of high-profile controversies, such as those involving BPA or PFOA, were insufficient to stimulate change. While under the right circumstances clear evidence of the TSCA's failure to even eliminate asbestos might have led to an update (perhaps a narrow one, for example, responding directly to the *Corrosion Proof Fittings* decision) even against the opposition of vested chemical interests, this did not occur in the immediate aftermath of the court's ruling.

---

[46] Downloaded from www.paint.org/aca-urges-congress-timely-resolution-tsca-reform/#sthash.BMALYb9J.dpuf.

[47] Nanotechnology involves the study and application of extremely small things, which are measured in terms of nanometers (the width of a hair is approximately 100,000 nanometers). Those concerned with toxics worry that nanomaterials may be more mobile and reactive than their larger counterparts, raising the question of whether they constitute new chemicals or not from a regulatory perspective.

By the mid-1990s, Congress had dramatically changed and gridlock and polarization prevailed. Net of a return to a low-polarization world where gridlock was less constraining and legislative cooperation far easier, the likelihood of substantially addressing the shortfalls of the TSCA seemed profoundly negative. And yet forces for change began arising from unexpected places.

5.1 Forces of Change: Above, Below, Outside

As foreshadowed, seeds for reform began being sown roughly midway into the first decade of the twenty-first century. The consensus opinion is that the most important change was the EU's promulgation of the REACH, whose implementation began on June 1, 2007, after approval a year earlier. Three features of the REACH are perhaps most notable relative to the TSCA (for an early comparison, see U.S. Government Accountability Office 2007):

(1) Burdens of proof are placed on chemical companies, rather than on the government à la the TSCA, to ensure that chemicals do not pose risks to human health or the environment;
(2) Chemical companies are required to lay out measures so that chemicals are handled and used safely, which was not a feature of the TSCA; and
(3) Information on chemicals was far more transparent than it was for the American regulations, with far less ability for producers to use the shield of CBI.

The sum of these differences for industrial chemical usage promised to be profound. Chemical firms would necessarily produce information, rather than rely upon benign ignorance (from their perspectives), and would have to institute a variety of safeguards if they wanted to get their products to market. In conjunction with a lesser ability to hide behind CBI protections, much information would be widely available so that not only EU government officials but other interested parties, even EPA administrators and environmental interest groups, would enjoy access. Clearly, therefore, chemical firms had new obligations that would reduce their compliance costs if progressive regulation in the United States was adopted, and many of the means that the industry had employed for minimizing the TSCA's impacts were threatened. While the REACH would take a long time to implement (its initial effects were only beginning to be felt in 2008, with full implementation planned for 2018; see European Chemicals Agency 2015), the status quo was shifting in a direction that qualitatively affected the strategic and competitive positions of chemical firms. Furthermore, with time the REACH increasingly became the standard not just in the EU but elsewhere, adding further headaches for the multinational chemical industry.[48] By the time of the Lautenberg Act's adoption, countries from Switzerland to Croatia and Serbia to Turkey had adopted or were adopting REACH standards.

As discussed briefly earlier, if this were insufficient, a number of states had also responded to the national government's inertia by taking matters into their own hands. The TSCA did not preempt American states from acting on their own. States – principally but not exclusively blue states – promulgated their own regulations. For example, states (with their percent vote for Barack Obama in 2012 in parentheses, which was 51.1 percent nationally) with ten or more adopted policies regarding toxics by mid-2016 (see Table 1) included California (60.2), Illinois (57.6), Maine (56.3), Maryland (62), Minnesota (52.7), New York (63.4), and Vermont (66.6), with roughly 100 more bills under consideration in state legislatures.[49]

---

[48] The United Nations has also been pushing to bring order to the multinational regulation of chemicals through its Globally Harmonized System of Classification and Labelling of Chemicals (e.g., Winder, Azzi, and Wagner 2005). The impacts of this program, while not as substantial, are essentially in the same directions as the REACH.

[49] And, indeed, many such progressive states argued vigorously against limiting their abilities to act through a TSCA reform. For example, the attorneys general of California, Hawaii, Iowa, Maine, Maryland, New Hampshire, New York, Oregon, Rhode Island, Vermont, and Washington sent a letter jointly to the Senate Committee on Environment and Public Works and the House Committee on Energy and Commerce opposing preemption (as did the governors of California, New Hampshire, Vermont, and Washington). Not surprisingly, attorneys general and other politicians from redder states correspondingly beat the drums for proposals with state preemptions.

Table 1 State Policies and Support for Obama Toxics in 2016 (Time of Lautenberg Act's Passage)

State	Number	Percent for Obama	State	Number	Percent for Obama
ALABAMA	0	38.4	MONTANA	1	41.7
ALASKA	0	40.8	NEBRASKA	1	38.0
ARIZONA	0	44.6	NEVADA	1	52.4
ARKANSAS	1	36.9	NEW HAMPSHIRE	1	52.0
CALIFORNIA	23	60.2	NEW JERSEY	2	58.4
COLORADO	1	51.4	NEW MEXICO	1	53.0
CONNECTICUT	8	58.1	NEW YORK	10	63.4
DELAWARE	3	58.6	NORTH CAROLINA	3	48.4
FLORIDA	0	50.0	NORTH DAKOTA	0	38.7
GEORGIA	0	45.4	OHIO	1	50.7
HAWAII	3	70.6	OKLAHOMA	0	33.2
IDAHO	0	32.7	OREGON	5	54.2
ILLINOIS	14	57.6	PENNSYLVANIA	1	52.0
INDIANA	2	43.9	RHODE ISLAND	4	62.7
IOWA	2	52.0	SOUTH CAROLINA	1	44.1
KANSAS	0	38.0	SOUTH DAKOTA	0	39.9

Table 1 (cont.)

State	Number	Percent for Obama	State	Number	Percent for Obama
KENTUCKY	0	37.8	TENNESSEE	1	39.1
LOUISIANA	2	40.6	TEXAS	0	41.4
MAINE	18	41.0	UTAH	1	24.8
MARYLAND	13	62.0	VERMONT	11	66.6
MASSACHUSETTS	3	60.7	VIRGINIA	2	51.2
MICHIGAN	6	54.2	WASHINGTON	9	56.2
MINNESOTA	10	52.7	WEST VIRGINIA	0	35.5
MISSISSIPPI	0	43.8	WISCONSIN	1	52.8
MISSOURI	0	44.4	WYOMING	0	27.8

Notes: Data on number of state policies from www.saferstates.org/; the support for Obama nationally in the 2012 election was 51.1 percent, meaning that thirty-two initiatives were from states with support below this percentage, and 134 were from states with support above it.

Many of these policies involved the specific chemicals already mentioned that were receiving public attention (e.g., asbestos, BPA, mercury, and PFOA), but others had greater breadth. Regarding the latter, for example, in 2008 California – the well-recognized leader in state efforts – enacted AB 1879, viewed as consciously mimicking the REACH. The law directed the state's Department of Toxic Substances Control to establish a process to identify and prioritize "chemicals of concern" in consumer products. With this process the Department was to determine how best to limit public exposure to these chemicals of concern and to reduce the level of hazard posed by the chemicals by the beginning of 2011 (for discussions of this so-called Green Chemistry Initiative, see Hsiao and Tarantino 2011; Chen 2012).

State policies greatly alarmed the chemical industry. They offered the prospects of continuous and costly political battles, myriad sets of rules having to be met on a state-by-state basis, continued regulatory uncertainty, and much stricter regulatory regimes. Secondarily, they could alert environmental groups that they should mobilize over toxics.

Also, state policies, as we see in what follows, greatly impacted the debate in Congress by disrupting standard ideological divisions. Most prominently, Democratic Senator Barbara Boxer, the leading Environment and Public Works Committee Democrat (chair when the Democrats were in the majority, ranking minority member in 2015–2016 when legislation was passed), proved a heavily obstructionist force. Boxer's opposition to changing the TSCA stands in contrast to ideological models that would predict that she would have preferred proposed alternatives to the national status quo as long as they were more liberal (e.g., Poole and Rosenthal 2007). Put differently, in dealing with the TSCA's reform, legislators such as Boxer found themselves allying with Republicans favoring the rights of states (on the tendency of the TSCA to create strange bedfellows, see Franklin and Reynolds 2012). While the latter wanted to limit the extent of industrial regulation in their states, the former's opposition and obstructive behavior were grounded on preventing states', such as California's, considerable regulatory efforts from being preempted by a brokered national agreement.

Finally, as mentioned, a third change in the world was the increased attention of societal interests seeking to pressure firms through shareholder resolutions, boycotts, and the like. In the name of social responsibility, these societal interests demanded changes in how firms used toxics directly as well as indirectly by firms in their supply chains. Not only were chemical companies under pressure, but numerous large US companies selling goods with chemicals found themselves being pushed as well. These pressures gave many companies incentives to support regulations (e.g., Berzon 2015). Numerous downstream users supported and actively lobbied for the TSCA's reform. (Such interests would also benefit from state preemption.) In practice, these actions had a forceful effect on chemical industry providers. Lobbying disclosure forms reveal a who's who involved in the political back and forth: Boeing, Cargill, the Dial Corporation, Disney, Ford, General Electric, General Motors, Hallmark, Hanes, Hasbro, Home Depot, Honda, Honeywell, Intel, S.C. Johnson & Son, Target, and Toyota are all members of this list – and this does not include mobilization by their trade associations (see also "Retailers, Chemical Users Weigh in on TSCA Reform" 2016).[50]

The upshot is that the status quo was moving beneath the feet of national political interests (e.g., DiCosmo 2013b). Change was less a function of administrative maneuvering at the national level and more a product of the political changes above and below and from outside the formal political sphere that could not be controlled or managed under the TSCA. In previous, low-gridlock times, a series of modest statutory changes given experiences and judicial decisions might have been enacted, making the situation later confronted less dire. Instead, the pressure and dissatisfaction with the status quo just kept building as the TSCA became more and more dysfunctional. The chemical industry's benefits from the TSCA, and the rewards to those relying on the industry for their products, were dissipating. While environmental interests saw the states and the EU acting on

---

[50] Lobby disclosure forms are filed with either the House clerk or the Senate secretary pursuant to the rules established by the Lobby Disclosure Act, as subsequently amended.

one hand, they remained dissatisfied with the national status quo on the other. *Polarization was creating a possibility for change.*

5.2   The Potential for Change

Thus, there was a deal to be cut that could make *both* industry and environmental interests better off (with the nuance that particularly active blue states might be somewhat dissatisfied): Harmonize regulations, often discussed in terms of providing regulatory certainty, and limit states in exchange for more restrictive, environmentally progressive, national regulations in the direction of the REACH.

The principal issue eventually became not the desire for revamped regulation but the ability of the key participants to work together. As discussed, there are always many possibilities for legislative obstruction. And, given the polarized political system, with congressional political parties and their respective group allies seemingly at war, legislators tend to engage in combat or to ignore contrary positions rather than to cooperate and to work toward forging compromises. To create the requisite majorities or supermajorities, political parties would need to organize collectively so that their members did not undermine the statutory process, or to at least not stop or punish members wishing to cross party lines in an effort to produce a successful piece of legislation; key legislators would have to hammer out an agreement attractive to both industry and environmental interests; a path would need to be found for moving proposals out of committees and onto the plenary calendars in a manner facilitating passage (e.g., without damaging amendments) and through the process by which chambers reconcile differing bills.[51]

In short, attempts to change policy administratively at the national level were insufficient given the realities that chemical producers and users and policymakers were facing. Only

---

[51] In the standard textbook depiction of Congress, this last step involves a conference committee comprised of House and Senate members, but such committees are rarely convened these days and were deemed less likely than coordinated negotiation to produce an acceptable reconciliation between the chambers for the Lautenberg Act.

a statutory action where an agreement was forged between chemical, business, and environmental interests, between Democrats and Republicans, had the potential to improve the situation markedly. Such a reform would involve limiting the states, moving toward the REACH's rules, and improving the reputational positions of producers and users of industrial chemicals.

To reiterate, that incentives to forge a new national policy existed did not mean that the sledding would not be rough. As former senior EPA official James V. Aidala, who has been embroiled in issues of toxics for decades, later put it as TSCA reform approached, "Congress has waited almost 40 years to do this [TSCA reform] because it's not easy to do it. Congress wouldn't be doing it if an administrative fix was possible" ("Dialogue: Toxic Substances Control Act Reform: What's Happening, and What's Next?" 2016, p. 10366).

6 The Bough Finally Breaks

> Chemical companies were finding their inability to satisfy their customers was starting to hurt their bottom line. It was becoming the Wild West out there, and they needed a sheriff.
>
> EDF Senior Scientist Richard Denison
> (cited in Drajem and Kaskey 2016)

> The American Chemistry Council and its members support Congress' effort to modernize our nation's chemical management system. Such a system should place protecting the public health as its highest priority, and should include strict government oversight. It should also preserve America's role as the world's leading innovator and employer in the creation of safe and environmentally sound technologies and products of the business of chemistry.
>
> American Chemistry Council ("Ten Principles
> for Modernizing TSCA" 2009)[52]

---

[52] Downloaded from www.americanchemistry.com/Policy/Chemical-Safety /TSCA/10-Principles-for-Modernizing-TSCA.pdf.

Thus, the stage seemed to be set for change. The world was evolving, politically from below (states and localities) and above (the EU and those mimicking it), and from outside the formal political sphere (nongovernmental organizations and citizens).

But high polarization and warring political parties meant that producing the cooperation required for generating a new statute, even when a majority or supermajority of legislators would appear to favor a potential compromise, could prove extremely problematic (e.g., Binder 2015). Settling upon which alternative out of the feasible set of choices preferable to the status quo is focused on and getting the requisite buy-in for change from those in positions to maintain even an unpalatable status quo was not assured.

6.1 Initial Attempts at Change: Decade of Failures

Despite the changes in the world at large, initial legislative efforts remained in statutory purgatory. With popular concerns, such as the impacts of BPA on fetuses and infants getting considerable attention from the citizenry and the states (on the impact of media attention on states acting on BPA, see Kiss 2013), and the TSCA continuing to be recognized as a failure, Democratic members of Congress began pitching reform starting in 2005. To make these proposals appealing they were typically spun as a means toward improving children's health (e.g., the "Kid-Safe Chemical Act"). However, such efforts made little headway, as business interests viewed them as slanted against their interests given the balance of what firms would be asked to do financially relative to what they would receive in return (note that the chemical industry still formally opposed reform, and that the REACH and state-initiated programs were only beginning to gain steam).

With the Obama administration assuming office in 2009 and other forces, such as the implementation of the REACH, making life harder for chemical firms, it might have seemed that the time for change had arrived (for an example of such optimism, see Service 2009). This would certainly be consistent with the typical view that

Table 2 Obama's and Jackson's Six Principles for TSCA Reform (2009)

1. Chemicals should be reviewed against safety standards that are based on sound science and reflect risk-based criteria protective of human health and the environment.
2. Manufacturers should provide EPA with the necessary information to conclude that new and existing chemicals are safe and do not endanger public health or the environment.
3. Risk management decisions should take into account sensitive subpopulations, cost, availability of substitutes, and other relevant considerations.
4. Manufacturers and EPA should assess and act on priority chemicals, both existing and new, in a timely manner.
5. Green chemistry should be encouraged, and provisions assuring transparency and public access to information should be strengthened.*
6. EPA should be given a sustained source of funding for implementation.

Source: U.S. EPA, Essential Principles for Reform of Chemicals Management Legislation, available at www.epa.gov/oppt/existingchem icals/pubs/principles.html

* Green chemistry is typically described as the production of chemicals that are nonhazardous across the life cycle (production, usage, and disposal).

environmental progress would most likely occur with a liberal president and a large Democratic majority in Congress. Indeed, some proclaimed that it was "now or never" (e.g., Greenwood 2009), while President Obama and his new EPA head, Lisa Jackson, both made clear that they thought that reform was desirable. To jump-start the process, in late 2009, the agency publicly issued six principles for reform (reproduced in Table 2), many of which should be intuitive given our discussion in past sections (e.g., providing sound standards, assuring the availability of information from industry, furnishing steady and sufficient funding, and prioritizing according to risk which chemicals are dealt with).

But, as is often the case, particularly in the modern world of polarization and partisan conflict, the path to legislation was laborious (e.g., Culleen 2015). Hearings in 2009 (U.S. House Committee on Energy and Commerce 2009) generated no proposal until April 2010, leaving little time in the 111th Congress before the November 2010 mid-term elections to produce a statute. Efforts spearheaded by Lautenberg made no dent in the partisan deadlock. Republicans exhibited no indications of breaking ranks, repeatedly voicing concerns about the economic costs and the negative impacts on innovation of updating the TSCA. The chemical industry, while not totally ruling out change, continued to express worries about the strictness of the decision-making standards being proposed. Specifically, it asserted that few chemicals would receive approval, that the negative impacts on innovation and the ability to keep production in the United States would be substantial, and that the provisions allowing continued state preemption and a lack of uniformity and regulatory certainty would be harmful.

As foreshadowed, strikingly, in August 2009, the industry took another significant step forward. Its trade association, the American Chemistry Council (ACC), formally came out as favoring reform. In doing so, the ACC proclaimed a willingness to furnish far more information than previously and a strong desire to reassure the public about the safety of chemicals (Layton 2009).[53] So, ironically, in the first year of a liberal Democratic president's term and with a heavily Democratic Senate and House,[54] the chemical industry

---

[53] This was not a complete turnaround for the chemical industry, which had already stated a preference for modernizing the TSCA but, rather, a change in degree of support (e.g., see ACC head Cal Dooley's testimony in the February 2009 congressional hearings; US House, Committee on Energy and Commerce 2009). The ACC, the chief industry spokes group throughout the reform process, also maintained that the efforts in the Democratic Congress were too extreme (e.g., wanting chemicals judged by whether they were hazards rather than by a less severe risk-based approach), with the majority party and its allies too emboldened by their perceived strong bargaining positions. This led some to question the industry's sincerity for change (e.g., the EDF; see Denison 2010).

[54] While numbers fluctuated a bit over time (particularly relevant for the Senate given the cloture number of sixty required to break a filibuster), for most of the Congress the Democrats Senate majority was 59–41 (including the two independents caucusing with Democrats) and their House majority was seventy-five or more seats.

reversed course. It supported the TSCA's reform despite almost certainly retaining an ability to work with its allies to maintain the statutory status quo (e.g., by simply keeping forty senators on its side to prevent any upper chamber action by maintaining a filibuster). Over time, as state and international regulation expanded, the industry would become more and more open to change (Tollefson 2016), helping facilitate bipartisan coordination and cooperation a few years later.

Still, the next Congress, far more Republican and even more polarized than its predecessor, with a much smaller Democratic majority in the Senate (fifty-three, again including the two independents caucusing with the party) and a large Republican majority in the House (forty-nine seats), failed to produce a breakthrough. There were suggestions of possible piecemeal reform that also did not gain steam. However, a foundation for the extremely difficult trick of getting polarized partisan interests to collaborate began to be laid. For example, representatives from Lautenberg's and Republican James Inhofe's (the ranking Republican on the Senate's Environment and Public Works Committee, and a notable climate change denier) offices met weekly. They alternated between bringing in environmental and industry representatives, trying to forge consensuses on specific topics. Republicans now controlling the lower chamber's agenda voiced support for the TSCA's modernization, industry stuck to its recommendation for change (i.e., continuing its support for reform even with Republicans holding a much stronger legislative hand), and the external forces impacting the induced preferences of business interests such as the implementation of the REACH and state preemptions continued. Yet the difficulty of polarized partisan forces working together led to continuing roadblocks and considerable sniping, for example between Inhofe and Boxer despite their close personal friendship. Democrats made statutory proposals to which congressional Republicans did not sign on given the specifics, such as the costs that industry was being asked to take on for chemicals' approvals (too high) and clauses about preempting the states (too weak).

6.2   Change Ultimately Comes: Passage of the Lautenberg Act

Finally, in the 113th Congress, the partisan tide began turning. As noted, in the background the EU's REACH program stayed on course in its development and implementation process (its five-year review in 2013 recommended continuing onward with no change in direction). Pressures from the states kept building with threats to pass new initiatives; such proposals were often combatted by the chemical industry at considerable expense, adding costs and complexity even when the initiative was successfully blocked.[55] Industry also continued to feel the impact of indirect forces. For example, to ramp up demand for statutory reform, environmental groups mobilized to pressure retailers like Walmart and Target to demand more benign products (DiCosmo 2013a). Both firms were pledging to clean up the chemicals in their supply chains at the time successor legislation was being considered, with Walmart crafting its chemical policy jointly with the EDF, the leading group pushing the TSCA's reform, and Target seemingly emulating Walmart's progressive changes to maintain its competitive position.

When taken in toto, these trends incentivized chemical producers and their major downstream customers to get a deal done to restore order and establish certainty. Thus, congressional Republicans started taking steps toward a solution by joining with Democrats. Notably, in May 2013 Louisiana Republican Senator David Vitter, the ranking senator on the Senate subcommittee, surprised many by collaborating with Lautenberg to introduce the Chemical Safety Improvement Act (Plautz 2013). The proposal was considered a groundbreaking attempt to forge a bipartisan TSCA reform. Even Lautenberg's death in early June

---

[55] As an example of the expenses involved with combatting these initiatives, in the third quarter of 2008, when the previously mentioned AB 1879 was passed in California, the American Chemistry Council alone reported lobbying expenditures exceeding $4.7 million (as compared to roughly $100,000 spent in the previous and subsequent quarters; data downloaded from http://cal-access.sos.ca.gov/Lobbying/Employers/Detail.aspx?id=1142931&view=activity&session=2007).

did not close the window on TSCA reform, despite some prognostications to the contrary. Led by New Mexico Senator Tom Udall, a leading proponent of environmental progressivity, Democrats began meeting with Vitter and outside groups (notably with the EDF and the ACC). In the House, Republican Representative Shimkus issued his own discussion drafts of potential legislation.

While by no means was the bill a finished product and many issues required intense negotiation, from the obvious (transparency, funding, use of CBI) to the more surprising (the increase in animal deaths from greater chemical testing, an issue of great concern to the American Society for Prevention of Cruelty to Animals [ASPCA]), agreeing on the extent of state preemption stood out. This was obviously a concern to chemical industry interests as well as, on the opposite side, to blue state environmentalists. The latter's preferences were most prominently represented by Boxer, who did not want to see her state's efforts as limited as the proposed Senate bill dictated. But not requiring such limits would obviously undermine some of the purpose of a new bill from the chemical industry's point of view. Boxer allegedly complained about this matter even on the plane trip carrying dignitaries to and from Lautenberg's funeral to the dismay of the late senator's widow,[56] and she later alienated her Republican committee counterparts by releasing a draft of a proposed compromise to the press that was supposed to remain confidential.

Time ran out for the 113th Congress to cut a deal. But, despite the discouragement of many involved, much of the spade work for a bipartisan agreement had been done (Pearson 2015b). Of course, interparty and industry–environmentalist collaborations would still not be easy.

The chemical industry was fully mobilized, working with Democrats and Republicans alike, as events were rapidly

---

[56] Bonnie Lautenberg told *Politico*, "It was horrifying to me because you have to understand the history: Frank Lautenberg and Barbara Boxer were very close friends. So, I was horrified and hurt, so hurt, when I heard that Barbara was bad-mouthing the bill on the way to his funeral, oh my God." www.politico .com/story/2015/11/toxic-chemical-bill-lautenberg-environment-21570

unfolding. Republicans took over the Senate with the 2014 election. In a key respect, Republican ascension actually improved the situation for an environmental bill, despite the party's usual skepticism of regulation. One consequence was that Boxer was no longer the committee chair as she was replaced by her Republican counterpart Inhofe, reducing her ability to keep TSCA reform off the plenary agenda (Pearson 2014; see, e.g., Cox and McCubbins 2005, for a discussion of such gatekeeping authority). So, while the California senator continued as an extremely vocal participant in the negotiations, focusing heavily on state preemptions as befit her California constituency, she no longer wielded the committee chair position as a tool as in the waning days of the 112th Congress. At least in this instance, divided government facilitated business cutting a deal.

With the chemical industry and many of its major users on board, and environmental groups such as the EDF heavily involved,[57] bills emerged from both chambers. The House moved first in June, with only one vote against, conservative Republican Tom McClintock of California, who cited the failure to reduce regulatory burdens on high-regulation states like his own.[58]

---

[57] Other environmental groups remained wary, particularly given issues of state preemption, although in the end virtually none of these organizations, Greenpeace being a notable exception, disputed that the final statute improved the status quo. Illustrative of a typical evaluation was the reaction of the League of Conservation Voters after the Lautenberg Act's passage:

For far too long, our nation's broken chemical law has allowed toxic chemicals into our homes and workplaces, contributing to a dramatic rise in health problems like cancer, infertility, and learning disabilities. The Frank R. Lautenberg Chemical Safety for the 21st Century Act will finally give the EPA the tools it needs to act on dangerous chemicals that are jeopardizing the health of our families and the environment.

While this law is clearly a compromise that includes rollbacks to state authority and the EPA's ability to regulate imported products, we commend those who worked so hard to improve it and ensure that it is an important step forward.

Downloaded from www.lcv.org/media/press-releases/LCV-Statement-on-Pres-Obama-Signing-TSCA-Reform-Into-Law.html.

[58] House leadership, including committee chair Shimkus, eased passage by using a procedure suspending chamber rules, thus prohibiting amendments

The Senate took another six months (via unanimous voice vote in December). Despite all the support for change, shepherding the Senate bill through was a particularly onerous task (for details, see Plautz 2015). Senate leadership (including Majority Leader Mitch McConnell), with presidential encouragement, initially assembled a clear filibuster-proof supermajority. These leaders subsequently paved the way to remove extra-statutory roadblocks involving energy and the previously discussed Land and Water Conservation Fund, prevented so-called fringe riders that could make the bill unacceptable to its bipartisan majority, then placated Boxer who was, in her own words, being a "pain in the neck" (Pearson 2015a), and finally allocated the requisite plenary time on a tight calendar to have a vote.

After passage came reconciling the bills' discrepancies. The House bill was less detailed than the Senate's almost 200-page offering. Although no formal pronouncements were made, the Obama administration and the EPA favored the upper chamber's bill (for example, as laid out in a letter from EPA head Gina McCarthy to ranking House Democrat on Frank Pallone on January 2, 2016, with the EPA carefully staying out of the preemption debate). Overall, the Senate's bill appeared more progressive than the House's in terms of setting deadlines for agency actions, specifying standards for evaluating existing chemicals, more generously funding the program, and laying out how new chemicals would be considered. The House's version was seen as more favorable only in its implementation requirements, but was viewed as more pro-business for issues regarding state preemption (which had been scaled back in April 2015 to win bipartisan support) and in dealing with chemicals contained in imported products.[59]

---

provided proponents could muster the required two-thirds support (which they knew that they had on an up/down vote). While some thought that the Senate was on a fast track to approval, it required considerably longer.

[59] Thus, while the EDF tended to favor the Senate's bill, the latter features led the progressive Safer Chemicals, Healthy Families alliance, an amalgam of environmental and citizens' groups, unions, and eco-businesses formed in December 2013 to represent sustainable business, to favor the House's.

Many observers expected that there would be a near instantaneous agreement reconciling the bills once the Senate acted, e.g., the *Congressional Quarterly* predicted action "sooner rather than later" on January 4 and continued for months with similar predictions of an imminent accord. Yet this was the not the case.[60] Rather, the process nearly ran out of time with a presidential election looming. (Given the victory of Donald Trump, it would be hard to prognosticate confidently what would have happened if reform had dragged into the next Congress.) Despite many pressures to get a compromise done (e.g., from the ACC, which mobilized a grassroots campaign via "Coatings Connect," and was part of a broad-based "Alliance for Innovation"), a variety of sticking points emerged.

Not surprisingly, the biggest issue involved state preemption, where a convoluted compromise was worked out between principal negotiators Inhofe and Boxer. Specifically, states' existing chemical regulations were grandfathered, so that they would remain in effect, but recent and new state requirements were blocked while the EPA reassessed chemical risks. States could not act while the EPA was evaluating the safety of chemicals and making a determination unless the agency took more than three and one-half years. However, preemption did not apply to the first ten chemicals that the EPA was directed to assess or to chemicals that firms requested for risk assessment so that they could enter the market. Given his opposition to taking away state's rights, libertarian-leaning Republican Rand Paul put a hold on the bill in late May (which could have been broken by a cloture vote given the overwhelming support). This made Paul and Boxer unlikely allies, although she had recently relented. Paul eventually backed off, ending his opposition on June 7.

Another frustrating sticking point involved safeguards on the amount of animal testing that would take place, an issue greatly concerning the ASPCA. This resulted in a standoff between New Jersey Democrat Cory Booker, who crafted compromise language,

---

[60] See "Environment: Toxic Chemicals Bill Nears Finish Line" (2016).

and in-state political rival Frank Pallone. Booker had defeated Pallone in the Senate primary to replace Lautenberg, and the lingering bad feeling from their electoral battle was thought to be influencing their standoff. In May, after much public pleading from fellow House members to fall in line, Pallone ceased opposing Booker's language and the bill cleared this hurdle.

An additional obstacle involved provisions for government promotion of green chemistry, the production of chemicals that are nonhazardous across the life cycle, which were in the Senate bill and championed by Delaware Democratic Senator Chris Coons at the seeming behest of Dow Chemical (which was merging with Delaware-based DuPont). This provision was eventually stricken in an effort to maintain broad support for the legislation and to keep other committees (notably the House Science, Space, and Technology Committee) out of the process.

Finally, the House passed the bill 403–13 on May 24, the Senate followed suit several weeks later on June 7 by voice vote after Paul withdrew his hold, and Barack Obama signed the Lautenberg Act on June 22. Red and blue in Congress had mixed together to produce green (Krupp 2016).

6.3   *The Secret of Success*

The Lautenberg Act was a rare legislative victory at a time when trying to pass meaningful statutes was typically a nonstarter. For example, even when Barack Obama allocated a great deal of political capital toward producing a cap-and-trade bill for greenhouse gases in the first years of his administration, the result was failure (Obama did, of course, succeed with the Affordable Care Act in 2010 during a brief period with a sixty-vote Senate Democratic majority). The status quo needed to be moved administratively.

As we have discussed, what made TSCA reform different was that a series of forces, not generally controllable by the national government, induced the chemical industry to come to the table and push for change that environmental progressives would buy into. This was the secret of success.

We should underscore, however, that, even then, change was an agonizing process, taking many years and with some ironies, such as the fact that Republican legislative victories appeared to ease coordinating on a compromise that could still be signed by Obama. The story of statutory policy change in our separation of powers system is always fraught with obstacles. Party polarization that severely impedes bipartisan coordination and cooperation makes success that much more subject to pitfalls and failure. Yet the Lautenberg Act became reality.

7 An Unexpected Twist: Implementation in the Age of Trump

> I am committed to implementing the Lautenberg Act as required by law including meeting the statutory deadlines enumerated in the law including the required rulemakings, risk evaluations, and future chemical prioritizations.
>
> > Questions for the Record for the
> > Honorable E. Scott Pruitt (January 18, 2017)[61]

> If we didn't remove incredibly powerful fire retardant asbestos & replace it with junk that doesn't work, the World Trade Center would never have burned down.
>
> > Donald Trump 2012 Tweet, Reported
> > in Kruse and Arrieta-Kenna (2012)

The enactment of a statute, commences, rather than ends, the process of changing policy and impacting societal welfare. With the TSCA's reform, the next step became implementing the Lautenberg Act's considerable requirements (see Figures 2 and 3 for descriptions for existing and new chemicals) and meeting its rather ambitious timeline (key deadlines are laid out in Table 3).

---

[61] Downloaded from www.epw.senate.gov/public/_cache/files/6d95005c-bd1a-4779-af7ebe831db6866a/scott-pruitt-qfr-responses-01.18.2017.pdf.

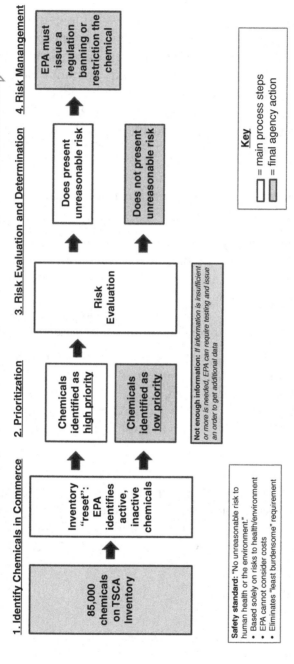

Figure 2 Process defined by Lautenberg Act for dealing with existing chemicals
Source: Denison (2017)

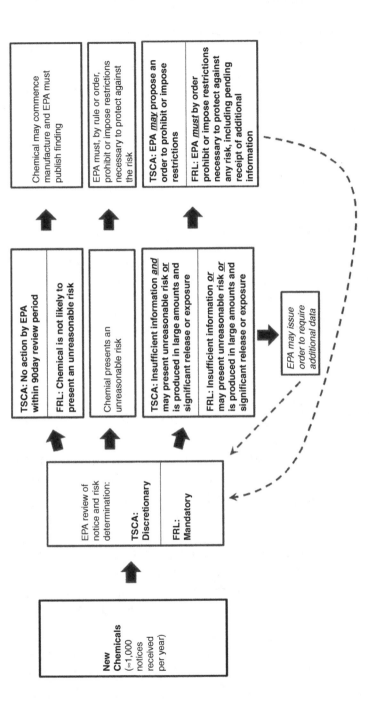

Figure 3 Process defined by Lautenberg Act for dealing with new chemicals
Notes: FRL = Frank R. Lautenberg Act; TSCA = Toxic Substances Control Act.
Source: Denison (2017)

Table 3 Key Agency and Manufacturer Obligations under the Lautenberg Act

Obligation	Time Frame
Agency to commence risk evaluations on first ten high-priority chemicals (from EPA Work Plan Chemicals list)	180 days
Agency to establish the process to identify additional high- and low-priority chemicals	One year
Chemical manufacturers must report to the EPA all chemicals they are currently producing or processing	One year
Agency to have risk evaluations under way for at least twenty high-priority chemicals	Three and one-half years
Agency to have completed risk evaluations	Three years, with possible six-month extension

7.1 A Tough Task

For a variety of interwoven reasons, the revised TSCA's implementation would be an arduous and probably conflictual process under routine circumstances of policymaking, particularly during the party-polarized era. But the circumstances of the TSCA's implementation would be far from routine, given the surprise (at the time of the TSCA's signing, at least) election of a president representing a dramatic break from the past.[62]

Regulating toxics is an inherently complicated process (e.g., Adelman 2010). Although the Lautenberg Act specified deadlines per Table 3, the tasks that were involved entailed great complexity and much discretion was left to the agency to implement them. Broadly, the overall authority delegated was to regulate the entire

---

[62] However, it was understood that implementation could be conditioned by whether a Democrat of Hillary Clinton's ilk or a Republican far more antagonistic toward environmental progressivity was occupying the White House.

industrial chemical industry far more effectively than previously, but not too intrusively. To begin, the EPA did not even know which of the roughly 85,000 chemicals were still in use. In addition, the EPA would be under pressure to deal with pent-up environmental demand over toxics competently and expeditiously, such as regarding high-profile concerns like asbestos (see DiCosmo 2016d). The agency was also faced with having to handle emergent new issues, such as those related to nanotechnology and synthetic biology (e.g., Davies 2008; Goldman 2009), layering additional complexities on the process. Thus, there was the real possibility that delegated responsibilities could prove daunting to the EPA, particularly relative to its capacities.

Indeed, there was concern from the very beginning about whether the EPA was up to meeting its responsibilities *qua* bureaucratic agency: whether it was, or could be made, sufficiently resourced and competent. For example, 325 new chemicals were in the queue waiting to get to market when the Lautenberg Act's passage necessitated a reboot. Could the agency deal with them quickly and efficiently? In terms of resources, while fees may cover up to 25 percent of implementation's costs (capped at $25 million for the first three years), not even the EPA's friends envisioned extra budgetary dollars beyond those monies.[63] Even presuming adequate funding, the agency could still lack the competence to pull off its considerable obligations (Szal 2016).

Related to these concerns, the agency's ability to deftly and effectively handle the extensive rulemaking for instituting the new regulatory regime would be crucial and demand considerable effort. Rulemaking routinely takes lengthy periods and is typically marked by conflict and legal challenges (for an overview, see

---

[63] EPA funding was a matter of concern (e.g., LaRoss 2016), but only the future will determine if it is sufficient or limiting. The initial budget authorization for the reformed chemical program was $56 million, which the agency implied would be enough for that time. The agency would accrue the aforementioned fees to cover one quarter of expenses, i.e., $14 million. Intriguingly, the ACC proclaimed that it would lobby for enforcement funds (which could help speed approvals), but whether Congress would agree to write the check was suspect.

Kerwin and Furlong 2010). Rules made under the Lautenberg Act would perhaps not go into force until 2022. Given the electoral calendar, implementation would necessarily occur along with the changing of presidential administrations, congressional turnover, likely upheaval in the top ranks of the EPA, and a possibly different relationship between the agency and the chief executive (Franklin 2016).

Also, conflicts were sure to arise between environmental and chemical advocates. Regulators would have to make choices between dueling interests, meaning that the EPA would need dexterity in balancing industry and societal concerns, including the voices of environmental and related state interests. For example, business opposition could arise if the costs that chemical companies were asked to bear in getting their products to market (e.g., in producing costly information and waiting without having the opportunity to reap back returns on investment) became too great or uncertain. Blue state politicians and environmental groups would undoubtedly push back on state preemptions to the extent possible, and chemical interests and their allies would respond in kind. Different interests would almost certainly bring court challenges seeking to define the boundaries of preemption limits as well as what uses would be considered in evaluating chemicals (e.g., current or potential future uses). Also, there would almost definitely be judicial challenges as a function of implementation on these issues and CBI (e.g., DiCosmo 2016a; Hegstad 2016).

Then there was the legislation itself. The Act, as with so many statutory outputs in a separation of powers system, was the culmination of a compromise between competing forces that left ambiguities that required hashing out. The contrasting interests that came together for the Lautenberg compromise had different objectives. Constructing a statute that would be politically acceptable to such diverse interests built in more hurdles than if it was simply authored by a policy analyst or enlightened social planner. While the authors of the Lautenberg Act tried to be precise in providing guidance and explicitly worked with the EPA to facilitate smooth implementation, disputes about matters of legislative intent looked likely to end up in the courts (e.g., DiCosmo 2016c). The intents of the House and of the Senate, as well as of Democratic and Republican supporters, could certainly be considered at odds, and there was no conference committee report to provide guidance for reconciliation (see Rodriguez 2016). Legal challenges could conceivably be as damaging as the *Corrosion Proof Fittings* ruling of yesteryear. Indeed, at the time of the Act's passage, the major question appeared to be whether the lawsuits would come prior to or after initial implementation efforts (for a discussion, see DiCosmo 2016b).

Further, as stated earlier, while the bough had broken once, the very forces that produced a forty-year gap between toxics statutes still existed and could potentially be relevant for implementation if new issues called for statutory action. Under current circumstances, Congress would not likely be able to adjust the policy statutorily given implementation experiences. With the many complicated facets of the policy, implementation may not all work out as envisioned or hoped for when the Lautenberg Act was enacted in June 2016. Although polarization and gridlock was overcome once, it was unlikely to be circumvented again to produce legislation building upon what was learned.[64]

If, for example, the courts rule something out of bounds, it is not likely that Congress would get its act together and address statutory interpretations or problems identified or created by the judiciary. Should one of the two polarized sides perceive an advantage from the ruling, it would probably block action and induce gridlock. Like most other policies during the high-polarization era, national chemical regulation will be back in the hands of bureaucratic drift, extra-statutory negotiations, and judicial rulings. Thus, despite the relief that polarization had finally been overcome, its persistence produced a great deal of caution and trepidation for future policy

---

[64] To reiterate, the REACH program had two five-year (known as REFIT) reviews designed to apply the EU's so-called principles of better regulation to update the regulations after implementation experiences. There was no equivalent for the Lautenberg Act.

effectiveness. Legislation promulgated under less polarized conditions could be adjusted more easily if the need arises.

In contrast to Congress's lack of ability to produce new statutes to help guide policy further, the Senate was more poised than in earlier years to approve appointees to influence the implementation process given that the filibuster was ruled out of bounds for appointments in 2013 (the so-called Reid rules change). Relevant political appointees doing the implementation could be more to the president's liking than in the past. This could be particularly the case if the president's party had a Senate majority, i.e., if the key fiftieth vote was from the chief executive's rather than from the opposition's party.

7.2 Business as Unusual

Of course, the world after the Act's passage was anything but business as usual. The twist distinguishing the Lautenberg Act's implementation was that, while the eventual bill was winding its way through the congressional labyrinth in the waning days of the Obama administration, Donald Trump was improbably ascending first to the Republican nomination and, four-plus months after passage, to the White House. To reiterate a point made in the Introduction, most experts viewed Trump's winning as a long shot at the time of the Lautenberg Act's enactment. There was scant discussion of it and no attempt to build in safeguards to shield the regulatory policy.

Yet Trump did triumph, with a victory that was, in a sense, the culmination of gridlock and polarization (e.g., Jacobson 2017). The political system had produced such extreme dissatisfaction among the voting populace that the ultimate outsider was first selected by a major party as its candidate and then went on to win the electoral college. This outsider was a virulent opponent of most environmental regulation and oozed disdain for the EPA. Although industry support for the Lautenberg Act protected it from wholesale attack, the new administration's effects on the law's implementation would likely be considerable.

Put differently, a Hillary Clinton victory would have presumably meant a reasonably smooth transition, with much continuity in the leadership assigned the very difficult task of implementing a new regulatory regime. Trump's rise generated more uncertainty given his lack of a track record and his pro-business, anti-EPA stance. He had routinely excoriated regulation generally and the EPA specifically and had largely questioned the need for environmental protections beyond assuring clean air and water (the issues traditionally of greatest concern to voters). Further, he had clear desires to cut the EPA's workforce and budget drastically, to make environmental regulation more business-friendly, and to populate the agency with a leadership responsive to his views. All of these efforts could potentially cause difficulties for new toxics legislation requiring a substantial expenditure; in 2016, the EPA predicted that each chemical review would cost $3.7 million and substantial effort and expertise.[65]

This long preamble leads us back to our third interrelated question: To what extent were environmentalists' hopes for chemical regulations dashed by the unexpected turn of events that they would be implemented by the Trump administration, with its general commitment to the so-called deconstruction of the American state? Certainly, Trump's earlier comments about asbestos, cited in the introductory quote to this section, as well as his overt hostility to the EPA throughout his campaign, gave environmental progressives reason for extreme wariness.

While the full rollout of the Lautenberg Act will take many years (and the author has no plans to wait), our discussion views the first eighteen months of implementation with these questions in mind. We delineate our analysis into two parts: (1) the immediate actions of the Obama administration and the EPA up until January 20, 2017; and (2) the subsequent choices of the Trump administration

---

[65] To reiterate, the authors of the Lautenberg Act anticipated that budgetary considerations could be an issue and stipulated that the EPA could collect up to 25 percent of its costs for administering certain parts of the Act (stemming from fees on manufacturer-requested reviews of chemicals), capped at $25 million a year for the first three years.

through calendar year 2017, with the latter receiving the bulk of our attention both because it encompasses a longer period and because the chances for policy conflict were far greater.

Although it might be surprising to those not sensitive to the forces that gave rise to the Lautenberg Act, but as the opening quote to this section from Scott Pruitt suggests, the new administration has not overtly tried to dismantle toxics regulation. While demonstrably more sympathetic to the chemical industry than its predecessor and antagonizing environmental interests along the way, it has not exhibited any inclination to launch a full-frontal attack on toxics regulation. Relative at least to its assaults on climate change legislation by defiantly rolling back Obama-era initiatives or its attempts to define navigable waters narrowly by rejecting the previous EPA's attempts to stretch what waters would be regulated under the Clean Water Act or any of a variety of other efforts, the new administration's impact on the Lautenberg Act's implementation is more muted and nuanced.

To this effect, the administration has focused on the specifics of rulemaking and the nature of relevant appointments. Even so, it is not clear that toxics regulation can be truly protected from the administration's broader attacks on EPA regulation beyond the Office of Chemical Safety and Pollution Prevention, as well as its attacks on the regulatory system in general. Nevertheless, Dimitrios Karakitsos, a senior Republican staff member of the Senate Environment and Public Works Committee (before switching to a lucrative lobbying job in the private sector) and a key player in negotiating the June 2016 agreement, opined that the revised "TSCA is not on the list of things they [those in the Trump administration] have gone after. I think the new administration would want to shape that policy rather than kill it before it goes forward" (quoted in Rizzuto 2016).

As we hope would be clear by now, the administration's disinclination to denounce and obliterate the new industrial chemical law is essentially a function of the same forces that produced the TSCA's reform in the first place. Thus, after a quick start to implementation in the Obama administration, the direct impact of his successor's EPA on toxics reform has been to manage, not to destroy, the law.

Not surprisingly given Trump's affection for asbestos, there is a more pro-industry focus than we might have seen out of a Hillary Clinton administration. There is nothing unusual about this, but the impacts have not been draconian. However, there is widespread worry – ironically, exacerbated by the Democrats' abolition of the filibuster for political appointments – that strong industry partisans are being brought in to run the relevant administrative efforts (although, as we see in what follows, the appointment perhaps most antithetical to progressives was beaten back). While it is too early to know definitively, the administration's general antipathy to the EPA could conceivably leave chemical regulation as collateral damage. If the EPA lacks the resources, both human and budgetary, to function effectively, contributions from other parts of the agency that will indirectly influence the implementation of the Lautenberg Act may be deleterious. This could be a function not of any desire to see the policy fail, but due to the broader efforts of deconstructing the bureaucratic state generally and the EPA specifically. By the same token, efforts to undermine the system of modern regulatory rulemaking could also prove debilitating.

Put differently, the Lautenberg Act, while not at business's ideal points – whether we are talking about the chemical industry or downstream users – was not passed over the objections of relevant economic interests. While these corporate concerns, part of the Trump constituency, might prefer this compromise bill to be implemented in specific ways, they do not advocate that the legislation be gutted. Furthermore, the processes outside the national level that had helped turn business opinions around have, if anything, gotten stronger (except to the extent that state actions are now limited by the Act's passage). The REACH and related chemical regulations are being implemented globally and pressures by nonprofits continue. The possibility that a more progressive administration could be in power in under four years might provide business interests with an incentive to install a policy that would be stable over time by not being too in favor of corporate interests at the expense of environmental progressivity and that, minimally, could pass judicial muster.

Indeed, we show here that these forces appear to be holding sway relative to anti-regulation zealotry.[66] For those opposed to Trump's campaign against the administrative state, there is hope that the Lautenberg Act will prove the positive exception to the negative rule, with the new policies being implemented while so many other environmental initiatives are being undercut.

7.3 A Quick Start: Implementation under Obama

The Obama administration did not take a breath upon the Act's enactment. Given how long the bill had been in the works, the EPA had many years to prepare for what it knew was a formidable task. The agency moved immediately toward implementation. Six days after Obama's signing of the legislation, the agency issued its first-year plan on June 28. By November 29, the EPA beat its deadline for identifying the first ten chemicals that needed to be reviewed. One was asbestos, despite the chlor-alkali industry's efforts to suggest that the chemical's employment was not problematic and that its modest commercial use should result in it not being in the top ten. Naming these chemicals triggered the requirements to have the

---

[66] Interestingly, there has been the expected Trump effect for chemical regulation that is *not* part of the Lautenberg Act. Most notably, the administration moved to delay implementation of a January 2017 EPA rule under the CAA, the Risk Management Program. The rule had been originally spurred on by a 2013 Obama Executive Order, finalized seven days before Obama exited office, and was set to go into effect in March 2017. The rule was disliked by the chemical industry, which had sent a petition asking for reconsideration within the first month of the new presidency. It was designed to tighten safety requirements, notably by publicizing information regarding what chemicals are being stored in large facilities. Trump referred to the national security risks associated with providing terrorists such information as motivation for his choice. Numerous environmental groups, including the Sierra Club, the Union of Concerned Scientists, and Earthjustice (the lead plaintiff), along with eleven mostly blue state attorneys general, sued the courts in classic modern environmental fashion, with their efforts proving unsuccessful.

reviews complete in the form of so-called scoping documents in three years and published in three and a half.

Keeping up this quick pace, the EPA had authored three proposed rules restricting specific high-risk uses of several chemicals and, most importantly, proposals for three key, more general, rules that it needed to produce under the law before the Trump inauguration in January. These rules covered (1) procedures for risk-based prioritization, i.e., how the agency will prioritize chemicals; (2) procedures for risk evaluation, meaning how the agency will conduct risk evaluations of high-priority and industry-requested chemicals; and (3) means of establishing fees to be collected from the industry to defray costs of administration of the Act (while this last rule had no statutory timeline it was essential for funding the agency's activities; see Environmental Protection Agency 2016). Finally, on January 19, as the moving trucks were pulling up to the White House, the agency clarified requirements for CBI claims under the new, more restrictive, dictums of the Lautenberg Act, an issue about which chemical interests were quite concerned.

In short, the Obama EPA moved speedily to deal with the TSCA, often in a manner causing some distress among business interests and with a general positive reaction from environmentalists. There was hope that these efforts would impact how the Trump administration would deal with the issue when the baton was passed.

7.4 A Bumpier Road: The Trump Transition

Not surprisingly, with the new administration there was a bumpier road and a somewhat less rapid pace but not a full-scale assault. In fact, environmentalists concerned with toxics regulation were cautiously pleased with the beginning months of the Trump administration. However, environmentalists' worries – and court cases generated by them – began to increase with time. Still, there was nothing akin to what was happening in most of the rest of the agency or any outright rollback of the regulation of industrial chemicals.

For environmental progressives, experiences could be grouped into positive, mixed, and negative.[67] On the positive side, there were no overt attacks on the program. As a precursor and a reminder of the bipartisan nature of the Lautenberg coalition, on November 30, 2016, nine senators, including Democrat Tom Udall and Republican James Inhofe, jointly wrote to President-elect Trump to urge that he "vigorously implement the new law." The new administration initially seemed to take heed. Notably, there was no effort to cut off resources to the Office of Chemical Safety and Pollution Prevention and in the spring, the administration claimed to be recommending a $14 million increase (the anticipated proceeds from chemical industry fees). By December 2017, the corresponding rule had been sent to the Office of Management and Budget for review. Moreover, despite worries, the agency continued to hit its deadlines as laid out by the new statute and by all accounts Scott Pruitt was engaged with the process. Rules were issued on time and the pace of new chemical reviews was on track.

The mixed news was the nature of what was coming out of the EPA once it got a chance to revisit the initial Obama proposals on chemical prioritization, risk evaluation, and CBI, essentially the "big three" rules that were released around the first anniversary of the Lautenberg Act's 2016 passage. All, as would be predicted, could be considered less pro-environment from the perspective of environmental advocates or organizations:

- As mentioned, the prioritization rule structures the process by which the EPA is to rate existing chemicals for their risks, including the criteria by which they are separated into high-priority and low-priority substances for risk evaluation. An important change to the final rule relative to the proposal made under the Gina McCarthy-led EPA was that the agency would identify the specific conditions of use that were the

---

[67] There is also likely to be a battle over how restrictive state preemption is, with the courts ultimately deciding. While some observers believe that such conflict is just on the horizon, perhaps over efforts in California to limit flame retardants, it has not occurred yet.

basis for the priority designation. While the initial proposed rule stipulated that all known, intended, and reasonably foreseen activities be considered, the final rule gave the EPA discretion to focus on uses likely to present the greatest concern. Thus, the agency would focus on ongoing or prospective commercial uses with respect to manufacturing, processing, and distribution. Features such as noncommercial and legacy (past) uses were generally excluded.

- As for the risk evaluation rule involving the EPA's assessment of the risks associated with a chemical's use, the key change made in the final relative to the initial proposed rule was that the agency, instead of having to consider all current and foreseeable uses of a chemical, could narrow its focus to those uses most likely to present an unreasonable risk. Another dispiriting change to environmental progressives was that the agency indicated that it could designate some uses as low risk before fully evaluating all potential uses.

- The industry notification or reset rule, intended to designate whether substances in the TSCA inventory were being actively used, covered CBI. Relative to the Obama EPA's initial proposal, the rule increased reporting exemptions, allowed less information on notifications, and delayed deadlines (for a discussion, see Franklin 2017).

These changes were disheartening to environmental interests and the predictable response, particularly given the inability of Congress to mediate statutorily, was to file lawsuits. Hence, Earthjustice took the lead for the first two rules, with the EDF spearheading the case for the industry reset rule. In each instance, other environmental interests joined the suit.

On the negative side for environmental progressives were three forces that did not directly involve policy choices but gave reason to worry about the future. The first was appointments. As mentioned, with no appointment filibuster and a Republican Senate majority, the Trump administration was poised to install well-known friends of the chemistry industry into leading positions. This roiled environmentalists. When Nancy Beck, the ACC's senior director of regulatory science, was named the deputy assistant administrator of the EPA's Office of Chemical Safety and Pollution Prevention in April, there was great outcry from the environmental community and sympathetic news media.[68] The Environmental Working Group vilified Beck as "The Scariest Trump Appointee You've Never Heard Of" (Benesh 2017). Environmentalists blamed Beck for helping to soften the key rules discussed earlier (for a detailed report of her efforts and influence that received a great deal of public attention, see Lipton 2017). Yet even more outcry was heard, with caution coming even from some Republicans, with the July 2017 nomination for assistant administrator of Michael Dourson. Dourson was a University of Cincinnati toxicologist who served widely as an industry consultant and whose research studies were analogized to disreputable studies produced for "Big Tobacco" (e.g., Kollipara 2017). Indeed, in December, with three Republican Senators voicing opposition and no Democrat stepping forward in support, Dourson became the rare Republican environmental nominee to step down (seemingly equally objectionable nominees for other EPA programs have been confirmed) and, as of this writing, no replacement had been announced.

A second factor worrisome to environmental activists involved what was happening in the EPA *writ large*. It was not clear whether the implementation of the Lautenberg Act could truly be siloed, so that what was going on elsewhere in the agency did not undermine it. It is hard to pinpoint how this has impacted what has occurred to date. Feared budget cuts and reductions in employment levels and institutional capacities will take a good while until fully felt (in 2018 Congress gave the agency a reprieve from Trump's proposed budget cuts, keeping funding at the previous year's level so that there was only a slight cut in real dollars, but employees with valuable scientific and institutional knowledge continue to flee without being replaced). Nonetheless, for example, there are concerns that reductions in the agency's computational toxicology research

---

[68] Her appointment did not require Senate approval.

budget could threaten the necessary testing techniques to implement the new regulatory regime (Hegstad 2017). More broadly, Richard Denison, the lead EDF scientist on chemical regulation, lamented that the "the notion that EPA could somehow neatly carve out one program area and keep it functioning well when the carving knives are rampantly slashing everything around it is, well, preposterous."[69]

Finally, efforts beyond the EPA to cripple the rulemaking process, so crucial for the new chemical policy regime's success, have worried those focused on chemical regulations. Proposals for a new Regulatory Accountability Act would dramatically slow down and likely mitigate the ability to use rulemaking, which is prescribed in the Lautenberg Act. To date, however, this proposed legislation is only a dark cloud on the horizon (although it has supporters such as the U.S. Chamber of Commerce), and its likelihood of getting through the legislative process seems modest, at least as long as the Senate filibuster continues.

7.5 Shielding Toxics

After the congratulations of passing legislation, the hard work of implementation begins. With the Lautenberg Act, there were many nuances. The forces producing the regulation represented an unusual moment of bipartisan and business/environmentalist cooperation for reasons that were largely external to Washington. To an extent, at least, this commitment continued into the implementation stage. At the same time, the most unusual of presidential elections took place, putting an overt opponent of environmental regulation in the White House, and the EPA and the larger regulatory system came under attack.

What has taken place has reflected both the cooperative success of the Lautenberg Act and the antagonistic thrust of the Trump

---

[69] Downloaded from http://blogs.edf.org/health/2017/04/10/where-theres-smoke-there-are-mirrors-the-trump-administrations-claim-to-preserve-tsca-implementation-under-its-proposed-epa-budget-is-pure-illusion/.

administration. Deadlines have been met, resources have been provided, although policies are more pro-business than they would have been given a more progressive presidency or Congress. The courts, as would have been expected under virtually any circumstances, are being drawn in. At the same time, the Trump administration's preference for personnel whose commitment to regulation is questionable and its general attacks on the EPA and the regulatory system constitute real threats. The Republican Senate's response to the first key nominee to implement the Act was unusually supportive of the law compared to others put up for the EPA during the same Congress.

In short, the answer to our third principal question is that the Trump effect on chemical regulation has been substantial, yet there have been tangible efforts to separate and protect industrial chemical policy from the general attack on environment regulation. The set of conditions that produced policy change in a time of stasis continues to be felt and to distinguish industrial chemicals policy from most others. While there is unhappiness on the part of environmental progressives, as one would expect with any conservative administration, and court cases will help determine how things play out, the deeper concerns are for what the future might bring.

8 Lessons Learned? Policy Success in an Age of Gridlock

This committee, especially the subcommittee, we just really had a pretty good successful run on reforming the TSCA. And I think it [Superfund reform] is somewhat similar. I think we all knew [the TSCA] program was broken. We all knew we could do better. And then that started the process.

Rep. John Shimkus, Chair, House of Representatives
Subcommittee on Environment and the Economy,
Committee on Energy and Commerce, July 13, 2016[70]

[70] Downloaded from http://docs.house.gov/meetings/IF/IF18/20160713/105195/HHRG-114-IF18-Transcript-20160713.pdf. See Yohannan (2016) for a discussion analogizing Superfund reform to the Lautenberg Act.

The Lautenberg Act was likely the greatest delegation of authority by Congress and the president to the EPA in four decades. Although it was a compromise policy not as comprehensive as the REACH, the agency's new ability to regulate chemicals could influence the products produced and consumed in virtually every sector of the American economy, impact what US companies export abroad, and influence perceptions of corporate social responsibility by NGO leaders, investors, and consumers.

For firms, the principal hope was that the regulatory certainty and harmonized rules needed to make good economic decisions were created and that the movement toward progressivism would enhance their reputations. Conversely, those with an environmental agenda looked for a good deal more protection from the ill effects of chemicals for the citizenry and the environment.

8.1 Answering the Questions

Having examined in depth the changing of the regulatory guard governing industrial chemicals, we now return to three motivating questions for investigating the Lautenberg Act: (1) Why was bipartisan support and inter-branch agreement between a Republican Congress and a Democratic president achieved? (2) Should the answer to the first question provide us greater optimism about the future for policy overall and for environmental efforts more specifically assuming continued polarization and gridlock? (3) To what extent was the implementation of the Act thrown off course by the largely unexpected rise of Donald Trump?

Regarding the first question, the Lautenberg Act saw the light of day due to a confluence of circumstances such that the costs of gridlock were so great that the bough broke. As political forces external to the national political scene changed the existing status quos in ways beyond effective administrative management, the relevant players preferred an alternative approach. Industry support for new legislation allowed legislators, their party leaders, and their group allies to coordinate and to overcome the numerous and time-consuming obstacles to change. The Act was not brought on by the type of major disaster that had often historically provoked policy change under less polarized conditions. For example, Superfund followed the Love Canal disaster, and the Toxics Release Inventory was a response to the nuclear meltdown at Three Mile Island. Change also did not come to be because existing policies were ineffective per se, which they were, or because of newfound scientific understandings or new chemicals being employed that might lead one to invoke the precautionary principle.[71] Policy failure had been recognized at least since the early 1990s and *Corrosion Proof Fittings*. At best, policy failure was a necessary but not a sufficient condition for change.

Rather, to recap, the key drivers of the policy breakthrough were (1) change induced by the EU via the REACH program, which was slowly being implemented and increasingly being adopted elsewhere; (2) more, and more vigorous, state efforts in response to national-level gridlock; and (3) pressure on corporations, both in the chemical industry and downstream, to behave in a more environmentally and socially responsible fashion. The first promised a world where firms would increasingly have to conform to far stronger regulations than they dealt with in the United States. These considerations reduced industry's estimates of the costs of compliance with US regulations at the same time as its expected costs for those dealing with different regulatory regimes went up. Also, as more information would be available to the EPA due to the REACH, the era of "ignorance is bliss" regulation for chemical firms was rapidly coming to an end. State actions were creating a dramatically altered landscape for chemical firms, which were being required to meet discrepant policies and subjected to unwanted uncertainty about what the future would hold. Based on a litany of new proposals under consideration each year as well as recent actions, such as those taken in California, the industry

---

[71] The precautionary principle is the notion that precautionary efforts should be made to protect against acts that potentially may harm human health or environmental quality even if relationships are not fully established scientifically. The burden of proof rests with the proponent of the act to prove that the negative effects do not exist.

expected that the future would become more taxing and perplexing for chemical firms and their downstream supply chains, not less. Furthermore, growing activism – seemingly spurred on by frustration with the inability of the national polity to act as well as many other factors – pressed for both industry reform and socially responsible investment. Given these pressures from private politics, the returns to exhibiting greater environmental consciousness were obvious.

Even with these processes at work, the path to change in an age of great polarization was arduous, taking more than a decade from its 2005 inception. Legislators, parties, and their leaders, so used to organizing collectively against each other rather than collaborating, found working together extremely problematic. The path to the Act took unintuitive twists and turns, such as the Republicans winning the Senate appearing to work in favor of changing the environmental status quo for the better, and strange alliances between climate deniers and progressives on one hand and liberals and states' rights advocates on the other.

This discussion foreshadows our answer to the second question, which, like so much of what we have detailed, is part bad news and part good news. On the negative side, we should not take the success of the Lautenberg Act's ultimate passage as evidence that we now have a general blueprint for change. Despite what Representative Shimkus opined, the reason that the TSCA was altered was that the status quo had effectively been changed from above, from below, and from outside the national political arena. New legislation did not result from policy failure, per se. In a formal theoretic sense, the status quo moved outside the gridlock interval (in that there were alternative proposals that had the potential to be sufficiently preferred to become law) *and* there were actors who were willing to pay the collective costs of organizing and mobilizing to steer its change through the legislative labyrinth. Much of the latter was probably a function of the uncertainty about the future and the lack of harmonized policies both proving very costly. For those aghast at gridlock and the state of many environmental policies, and seeking a blueprint for the statutory overhaul of environmental policy generally, our findings are disappointing.

For environmental policy, or for other policy areas for that matter, there will need to be far more than a history of failure to achieve desired outcomes. Whether it be Superfund, the Endangered Species Act, the management of nonpoint water pollution, or some other consideration, change will remain the province of drift generated by the combination of extra-statutory pressures, administrative and executive choices, and judicial responses. Also, we have suggested that the confluence of circumstances and the difficulty in facilitating coordination necessary for TSCA reform potentially bodes poorly for the Act's implementation if subsequent statutory action is needed in the future. Given the complexities involved and the vagaries of judicial decisions, it should not surprise us if this were the case. Although prognostication is always tricky, polarization and gridlock are likely to reassert themselves.

Conversely, these obstacles do *not* mean that all is lost and we will never witness changes that are analogous to that of the Lautenberg Act. The world is growing ever more integrated economically, and the United States is no longer at the cutting edge for environmental progressivity specifically (this title now belongs to the EU). The American states remain highly divided, with blue states often trying to do what the national government will not. And private pressures on firms and industries have continued to ratchet up.

Thus, we can foresee the same circumstances that produced the Lautenberg Act inducing other national statutes as well. For example, it is possible to imagine automobile companies, in alliance with their large down-market consumers (e.g., FedEx or UPS), working with environmentalists to get national-level legislation that facilitates electric vehicle development and production, limits states setting up their own regulatory regimes, and corresponds more with rules abroad for reasons roughly corresponding to those behind the TSCA's reform. This is because there are a variety of pressures pushing auto producers toward developing their electric offerings: international pressures from the EU and others (e.g., China); regulatory actions in California that have been adopted by numerous other, mostly blue, states; and advocates of corporate social responsibility such as the EDF pushing automakers and those downstream. Indeed, the difficulty automobile manufacturers face in dealing with this confluence of forces is very much behind their dramatic increases in investments in electric vehicles of late, which is likely to make them that much more amenable to progressive regulatory initiatives in the future (e.g., Carey and White 2018 on Ford's choices).

We can imagine similar scenarios for any number of other environmental issues – genetically modified organisms, elements of climate change, etc. Furthermore, this same logic could extend to other issue areas as well. For example, consider the regulation of pharmaceuticals, which are just other types of chemicals. Despite the importance of the Food and Drug Administration at the national level, pharmaceuticals are subject to numerous different state rules as well (for an overview, see Schneider 2016). Drug firms are multinational concerns that face very different regulatory regimes, for example between the United States and Europe (for an overview, see Van Norman 2016). Drug companies, "Big Pharma," also face similar pressures from the private political forces that we have detailed. As such, we could imagine a confluence of circumstances that could produce a similar deal to the Lautenberg Act. There could be more progressive regulations, state limitations, more cross-national consistency, and rehabilitation of firm reputations.

Turning to our final question, the ascendance of Donald Trump has had an impact but, due to the reasons the Lautenberg Act was passed in the first place, seemingly not as dramatic, as anti-regulation, as anti-environmental progressivity, as we might otherwise expect. Deadlines have been met, funds are available, and there is some Republican push to move things along and to guard the appointments process. The external realities are that the REACH will not disappear, blue states, while more restricted, will continue to push the boundaries, and the business community will remain under nonmarket pressures. All of these realities assist with implementation, just as they drove the passage of the law in the first place. However, the Trump administration has pushed policies in the expected conservative direction, with the courts likely serving as an important arbiter. The Trump effect also will be almost certainly somewhat greater due to the Reid rules that eliminated the need for supermajorities in the Senate for successful appointments. Finally, it remains an open question whether the Act's implementation will suffer unintended, collateral damage given the general efforts being made to undo environmental regulation specifically and regulation generally.

Still, our analysis suggests that if statutory success can be realized, the willingness to implement may be greater than is the norm. Without such implementation, many of the positive expectations from statutory change for both sides will remain unrealized.

8.2 Final Thoughts

The Lautenberg Act was an extraordinary event. It provided our initial motivation to find out how environmentally progressive legislation could somehow be produced in a world that seemed ossified, polarized, and gridlocked – how the proverbial bough broke – and whether this occurrence provided some dramatic insight into how such stasis could be overcome. What we found was more nuanced than a single dramatic insight.

What we uncovered was a set of circumstances that induced changes as a product of gridlock, given that the larger world could not be controlled. Changes in the external environment altered incentives and brought warring interests to the negotiating table. With the rise of Donald Trump, we saw that the reasons for change made the treatment of industrial chemicals by the new administration somewhat unique though, at the same time, the regulatory policy was not immune from presidential and corresponding congressional influences. Additionally, the new administration might not be able, or be particularly disposed, to shield such policies from its larger onslaughts on the EPA and the regulatory system *writ large*.

For environmental progressives or for those who want to see gridlock overcome and policy issues addressed by the body politic, the regulation of industrial chemicals does not offer a roadmap for policy change generically. Rather, it demonstrates the *possibility of change* if certain conditions are met and the stars align. These circumstances might become more and more common with continued polarization and gridlock. States are increasingly prone to take things into their own hands, global trade and integration more and more tie regulatory impacts together, and the reputational pressures on firms and industries seem to grow unabated. The experience with the Lautenberg Act also underscores that, with some nuances, in the end commitment to implementation may be greater when we do realize statutory creation, as both business and societal interests will have a greater commitment to seeing policy move forward.

Acknowledgements

I would like to thank the staff at Cambridge University Press and, especially, Frances Lee for two careful readings of the manuscript as the Elements editor. Jeffrey Lewis and Keith Poole generously provided the data on polarization and Richard Dennison of the Environmental Defense Fund allowed me to reproduce several of his illuminating figures. The Chemical Heritage Foundation was very helpful in providing access to their oral histories and securing permission for their usage when necessary.

This manuscript reflects a personal interest in environmental policy that has been strengthened and reinforced over three decades by my undergraduate students at the University of Rochester and by MBA students during my tenure at the Kellogg School at Northwestern. I dedicate my Element to these generations of students and their collective enthusiasm, wisdom, and curiosity.

References

Adelman, D. E. (2010). A cautiously pessimistic appraisal of trends in toxics regulation. *Washington University Journal of Law & Policy*, 32(1): 377–442.

Adler, J. H., ed. (2011). *Rebuilding the Ark: New Perspectives on Endangered Species Act Reform*, Washington, DC: American Enterprise Institute.

Anderson, S. E. (2012). Policy domain-specific ideology: When interest group scores offer more insight. *Politics & Policy*, 40(6): 1186–1202.

Applegate, J. S. (2008). Synthesizing TSCA and REACH: Practical principles for chemical regulation reform. *Ecology Law Quarterly*, 35(4): 721–769.

Applegate, J. S., J. G. Laitos, J. M. Gaba, and N. M. Sachs. (2011). *The Regulation of Toxic Substances and Hazardous Wastes*, 2nd edn, New York: Foundation Press.

Auer, C. M., F. D. Kover, J. V. Aidala, and M. Greenwood. (2016). *Toxic Substances: A Half Century of Progress*, Washington, DC: EPA Alumni Association.

Barber, M., and N. McCarty. (2015). Causes and consequences of polarization. In N. Persily, ed., *Solutions to Political Polarization*. New York: Cambridge University Press, pp. 15–58.

Baron, D. P. (2003). Private politics. *Journal of Economics & Management Strategy*, 12(1): 31–66.

Benesh, M. (2017). The scariest Trump appointee you've never heard of. Environmental Working Group, May 2, www.ewg.org/planet-trump/2017/05/scariest-trump-appointee-you-ve-never-heard#.WeT94mhSyUl.

Bergeson, L. L. (2016). *The New and Improved TSCA: An Overview of Key Provisions in the Amended TSCA*, Chicago: American Bar Association.

Bergeson, L. L., L. M. Campbell, and L. Rothenberg. (2000). TSCA and the future of chemical regulation. *Environmental Law Reporter*, 15(4): 1–23.

Berzon, A. (2015). Chemical firms encourage more U.S. regulation. *Wall Street Journal*, Dec. 22, p. B1.

Binder, S. (2015). The dysfunctional Congress. *Annual Review of Political Science*, 18: 85–101.

Binder, S. (2017). Polarized we govern? In A. S. Gerber and E. Schickler, eds., *Governing in a Polarized Age: Political Representation in America*. New York: Cambridge University Press, pp. 223–242.

Boyd, J., and R. Epanchin-Niell. (2017). Private sector conservation investments under the Endangered Species Act: A guide to return on investment analysis. Resources for the Future, discussion paper 17–11.

Bryner, G. C. (1993). *Blue Skies, Green Politics: The Clean Air Act of 1990*, Washington, DC: Congressional Quarterly Press.

Callander, S., and K. Krehbiel. (2014). Gridlock and delegation in a changing world. *American Journal of Political Science*, 58(4): 819–834.

Callander, S., and G. J. Martin. (2017). Dynamic policymaking with decay. *American Journal of Political Science*, 61(1): 50–67.

Carey, N., and J. White. 2018. Ford plans $11 billion investment, 40 electrified vehicles by 2022. Reuters, Jan. 14. www.reuters.com/article/us-autoshow-detroit-ford-motor/ford-plans-11-billion-investment-40-electrified-vehi cles-by-2022-idUSKBN1F30YZ.

Carpenter, D., and D. A. Moss. (2013). *Preventing Regulatory Capture: Special Interest Influence and How to Limit It*, New York: Cambridge University Press.

Chen, P. J. (2012). Navigating California's REACH, aka, the Green Chemistry Initiative. *Natural Resources & Environment*, 26(4): 34–36.

Chiou, F.-Y., and L. S. Rothenberg. (2017). *The Enigma of Presidential Power: Parties, Policies, and Strategic Uses of Unilateral Action*, New York: Cambridge University Press.

Congressional Budget Office. (2015). *Cost Estimate: S. 697 Frank R. Lautenberg Chemical Safety for the 21st Century Act*, Washington, DC: Congressional Budget Office.

Council on Environmental Quality. (1971). *Toxic Substances*, Washington, DC: Council on Environmental Quality.

Cox, G. W., and M. D. McCubbins. (2005). *Setting the Agenda: Responsible Party Government in the U.S. House of Representatives*, New York: Cambridge University Press.

Culleen, L. E. (2015). Removing the roadblocks to TSCA reform. *Natural Resources & Environment*, 29(4): 3–6.

Davies, J. C. (2008). *Nanotechnology Oversight: An Agency for the New Administration*, Washington, DC: Woodrow Wilson Center.

Deacon, D. T. (2016). Administrative forbearance. *Yale Law Journal*, 125(6): 1548–1614.

Denison, R. A. (2009). Ten essential elements in TSCA reform. *Environmental Law Reporter*, 39(1): 10020–10028.

Denison, R. A. (2010). Not playing nice: The American Chemistry Council solidifies its claim to being the "industry of no," Washington, DC: Environmental Defense Fund. http://blogs.edf.org/health/2010/07/30/not-playing-nice-the-american-chemistry-council-solidifies-its-claim-to-being-the-industry-of-no/.

Denison, R. A. (2017). A primer on the new Toxic Substances Control Act and what led to it, Washington, DC: Environmental Defense Fund. www.edf.org/sites/default/files/denison-primer-on-lautenberg-act.pdf

Dialogue: Toxic Substances Control Act reform: What's happening, and what's next? (2016). *Environmental Law Reporter*, 46(5): 10357–10368.

DiCosmo, B. (2013a). Environmentalists pressure retailers in bid to boost leverage in TSCA talks. *InsideEPA.com's Daily Briefing*, Oct. 25 (online).

DiCosmo, B. (2013b). EPA studies, California rules may guide "risk" level absent TSCA reform. *Inside EPA Weekly Report*, 34(7), Feb. 15 (online).

DiCosmo, B. (2016a). Courts likely to address TSCA reform "cost-effectiveness" requirement. *InsideEPA.com's Daily Briefing*, June 29 (online).

DiCosmo, B. (2016b). Doubts linger on EPA's ability to swiftly ban asbestos under TSCA law. *Inside EPA Weekly Report*, 37(27), July 8 (online).

DiCosmo, B. (2016c). GOP senators at odds with Democrats on intent for TSCA bill provisions. *Inside EPA's Environmental Policy Alert*, 33(13), June 22 (online).

DiCosmo, B. (2016d). TSCA supporters say lawsuits will likely hinge on EPA's implementation. *Inside EPA Weekly Report*, 37(27), July 8 (online).

Drajem, M., and J. Kaskey. (2016). DuPont, Dow to get what they asked for: Tough EPA oversight, *Bloomberg Politics* (online).

Duval, M. (1975). Memorandum for the president: Environmental message, Gerald R. Ford Library, Feb. 12.

Environment: Toxic Chemicals Bill Nears Finish Line. (2016). *CQ Weekly*, Jan. 4 (online).

Environmental Defense Fund. (2009). *Across the Pond: Assessing REACH's First Big Impact on U.S. Companies and Chemicals*, updated version, Washington, DC: Environmental Defense Fund.

Environmental Protection Agency. (2016). *The Frank R. Lautenberg Chemical Safety for the 21st Century Act: First Year Implementation Plan*, Washington, DC: Environmental Protection Agency.

Environmental Protection Agency. (2017). *Superfund Task Force Recommendations*, Washington, DC: Environmental Protection Agency.

European Chemicals Agency. (2015). *ECHA's REACH 2018 Roadmap*, Helsinki: European Chemicals Agency.

Everts, S. (2012). Jody Roberts: The science historian discovers flaws in original design and implementation of much debated Toxic Substances Control Act. *Chemical & Engineering News*, 90(8): 38.

Filipec, O. (2017). *REACH beyond Borders: Europeanization towards Global Regulation*, Cham: Springer Nature.

Flippen, J. B. (2006). *Conservative Conservationist: Russell E. Train and the Emergence of American Environmentalism*, Baton Rouge: Louisiana State University Press.

Frankel, J. (2014). *The Rise and Fall of Cap-and-Trade*, Cambridge, MA: Belfar Center, Harvard University, Feb. 18. www.belfercenter.org/pub lication/rise-and-fall-cap-and-trade.

Franklin, C., and A. Reynolds. (2012). TSCA reform and preemption: A walk on the third rail. *Natural Resources & Environment*, 27(1): 14–18.

Franklin, K. (2016). EPA implementation of TSCA to be "enormous undertaking." *Chemical Watch*, June 16 (online).

Franklin, K. (2017). Final TSCA inventory notification rule eases reporting burden. *Chemical Watch*, June 29 (online).

Freeman, J. (2015). Why I worry about UARG. *Harvard Environmental Law Review*, 39(1): 9–22.

Freeman, J., and D. B. Spence. (2014). Old statutes, new problems. *University of Pennsylvania Law Review*, 163(1): 1–93.

Gamper-Rabindran, S., and S. R. Finger. (2013). Does industry self-regulation reduce pollution? Responsible Care in the chemical industry. *Journal of Regulatory Economics*, 43(1): 1–30.

Gelman, A. (2009). *Red State, Blue State, Rich State, Poor State: Why Americans Vote the Way They Do*, expanded edn, Princeton, NJ: Princeton University Press.

Goldman, L. R. (2009). Toxic chemicals and pesticides: Not yet preventing pollution. In J. C. Dernbach, ed., *Agenda for a Sustainable America*, Washington, DC: ELI Press, pp. 305–320.

Goldman, L. R. (2015). *Written Testimony: Frank R. Lautenberg Chemical Safety for the 21st Century Act*, Washington, DC: U.S. Senate Environment and Public Works Committee.

Greenwood, M. A. (2009). TSCA reform: Building a program that can work. *Environmental Law Reporter*, 39(1): 10034–10041.

Greve, M. S., and A. C. Parrish. (2015). Administrative law without Congress. *George Mason Law Review*, 22(3): 501–547.

Grossmann, M. (2014). *Artists of the Possible: Governing Networks and American Policy Change since 1945*, New York: Oxford University Press.

Hacker, J. S. (2004). Privatizing risk without privatizing the welfare state: The hidden politics of social policy retrenchment in the United States. *American Political Science Review*, 98(2): 243–260.

Hanshaw, R. (2015). Regulation of nanomaterials: What are they? How are they regulated? *Natural Resources & Environment*, 29(4): 44–47.

Hegstad, M. (2016). Attorneys say proposed TSCA rule may violate trade secret provisions. *Inside EPA Weekly Report*, 37(34), Aug. 26 (online).

Hegstad, M. (2017). FY18 cuts to EPA comptox research could hinder TSCA implementation. *Inside EPA Weekly Report*, 38(23), June 9 (online).

Hopkinson, J. (2012). U.S.–EU trade plans pose challenge to industry on TSCA reform efforts. *Inside EPA's Environmental Policy Alert*, 29(26), Dec. 26 (online).

Howell, W. G., and T. M. Moe. (2016). *Relic: How Our Constitution Undermines Effective Government – and Why We Need a More Powerful Presidency*, New York: Basic Books.

Hsiao, P., and W. F. Tarantino. (2011). California's Green Chemistry initiative. *Trends: ABA Section of Environment, Energy, and Resources Newsletter*, 42(4): 8–9.

Hull, S., J. Kou, and D. L. Spar. (1996). Union Carbide's Bhopal Plant (A), Harvard Business School Case 795070.

Humphreys, G. W. (1976). Memorandum to Jim Cavanaugh: Proposed outline for environmental speech. Gerald R. Ford Library, March 16.

Jacobson, G. C. (2017). The triumph of polarized partisanship in 2016: Donald Trump's improbable victory. *Political Science Quarterly*, 132(1): 9–41.

Judy, M. L., and K. N. Probst. (2009). Superfund at 30. *Vermont Law Review*, 11(2): 191–247.

Kerwin, C. M., and S. R. Furlong. (2010). *Rulemaking: How Government Agencies Write Law and Make Policies*, 4th edn, Washington, DC: CQ Press.

King, A. A., and M. J. Lennox. (2000). Industry self-regulation without sanctions: The chemical industry's Responsible Care program. *Academy of Management Journal*, 43(4): 698–716.

Kiss, S. J. (2013). Legislation by agenda-setting: Assessing the media's role in the regulation of bisphenol A in the U.S. States. *Mass Communication and Society*, 16(5): 687–712.

Klyza, C. M., and D. J. Sousa. (2013). *American Environmental Policy: Beyond Gridlock*, 2nd edn, Cambridge, MA: MIT Press.

Kollipara, P. (2017). Controversy greets Trump pick to lead EPA chemical safety programs. *Science*, July 21 (online).

Krupp, F. (2016). When red and blue in Congress makes green. *Wall Street Journal*, June 10, p. A13.

Krupp, F. (2017). Trump and the environment: What his plans would do. *Foreign Affairs*, 96(4): 73–82.

Kruse, M., and R. Arrieta-Kenna. (2016). The 7 oddest things Donald Trump thinks. *Politico*, Oct. 13 (online).

LaRoss, D. (2015). Potential FY16 bill rider on LWCF could free TSCA reform bill for vote. *Inside EPA Weekly Report*, 36(49), Dec. 11 (online).

LaRoss, D. (2016). Udall says EPAs' funding adequate to start implementing TSCA reform. *Inside EPA's Environmental Policy Alert*, 33(13), June 22 (online).

Lazarus, R. J. (2014). Environmental law without Congress. *Journal of Land Use & Environmental Law*, 30(1): 15–34.

Lazarus, R. J. (2015). Judicial missteps, legislative dysfunction, and the public trust doctrine: Can two wrongs make a right? *Environmental Law*, 45(4): 1139–1162.

Lee, F. E. (2015). How party polarization affects governance. *Annual Review of Political Science*, 18: 261–282.

Lerner, S. (2016). A chemical shell game: How DuPont concealed the dangers of the new Teflon toxin. *The Intercept*, https://theintercept.com/2016/03/03/how-dupont-concealed-the-dangers-of-the-new-teflon-toxin/.

Lipton, E. (2017). Trump rules: Why has the E.P.A. shifted on toxic chemicals? An industry insider helps call the shots. *New York Times*, Oct. 22, p. A1.

Liroff, R. A. (2008). Product toxic lockout. *The Environmental Forum*, 25 (3): 28–33.

Lovell, A. (2010). Environmentalists see new state, EU rules driving TSCA reform in 2011. *Inside EPA's Risk Pol Environmental Policy Alert*, 27(23), Nov. 17 (online).

Markell, D. (2010). An overview of TSCA, its history and key underlying assumptions, and its place in environmental regulation. *Washington University Journal of Law & Policy*, 32(1): 333–375.

McCarty, N., K. T. Poole, and H. Rosenthal. (2016). *Polarized American: The Dance of Ideology and Unequal Riches*. Cambridge, MA: MIT Press.

McCubbins, M. D., R. G. Noll, and B. R. Weingast. (1987). Administrative procedures as instruments of political control. *Journal of Law, Economics & Organization*, 3(2): 243–277.

Molander, L., and A. K. Cohen. 2012. EU and US regulatory approaches to information on chemicals in products: Implications for consumers. *European Journal of Risk Regulation*, 3(4): 521–533.

Nicoll, Don. (1999). Interview with Russell Train. Edmund S. Muskie Oral History Collection, Lewiston, ME: Bates College.

Orbach, B. (2013). What is government failure? *Yale Journal on Regulation*, 30 (online).

Organisation for Economic Co-operation and Development (OECD). (2012). *OECD Environmental Outlook to 2050: The Consequences of Inaction*, Paris: OECD Publishing.

Pearson, S. (2014). Industry groups expect better odds for TSCA changes with Boxer in diminished role, though path to 60 votes is not clear. *Greenwire*, Nov. 7 (online).

Pearson, S. (2015a). Being a "pain in the neck" worth it in TSCA fight – Boxer. *Greenwire*, Dec. 3 (online).

Pearson, S. (2015b). Key lawmakers eye continued negotiations for compromise TSCA update. *Greenwire*, Jan. 12 (online).

Plautz, J. (2013). Lautenberg and Vitter announce surprise bipartisan TSCA bill. *Greenwire*, May 22 (online).

Plautz, J. (2014). Why Congress can't fix our crazy chemical safety system. *National Journal Daily A.M.*, May 1 (online).

Plautz, J. (2015). The Senate finally passed chemical safety reform. Here's how they did it. *National Journal*, Dec. 18 (online).

Plautz, J. (2016). Why toy companies, automakers, and the oil industry want more EPA power. *National Journal Daily A.M.*, May 24 (online).

Poole, K. T., and H. Rosenthal. (2007). *Ideology and Congress*, 2nd edn, Piscataway, NJ: Transaction Publishers.

Rabkin, J. A. (2013). Against the EPA, absurdity is no defense. *Harvard Journal of Law and Public Policy*, 37(1): 41–48.

Reichley, A. J. (1976). Memorandum to Dick Cheney: Constituency Analysis. Gerald R. Ford Library, June 25.

Responsible Care Advisory Panel. (2011). *Report to the American Chemistry Council's Board Committee on Responsible Care*, Washington, DC: Responsible Care.

Retailers, chemical users weigh in on TSCA reform. (2016). *Bloomberg BNA*, May 9 (online).

Rissman, A. R., and S. R. Carpenter. (2015). Progress on nonpoint pollution: Barriers & opportunities. *Daedalus*, 144(3): 35–47.

Rizzuto, P. (2016). Trump's pick to lead EPA supported changes to chemical law. *Bloomberg BNA*, Dec. 23.

Rodriguez, J. C. (2016). TSCA reform's success rests on EPA's shoulders. *Law360* (online).

Russell, M. (1976a). Conferees agree on regulation of toxic chemicals. *Washington Post*, Sept. 15, p. A2.

Russell, M. (1976b). Ford signs bill on toxic substances. *Washington Post*, Oct. 3, p. A3.

Schierow, L.-J. (2009). The Toxic Substances Control Act (TSCA): Implementation and New Challenges. Congressional Research Service Report RL34118.

Schierow, L.-J. (2013). The Toxic Substances Control Act (TSCA): A Summary of the Act and Its Major Requirements. Congressional Research Service Report RL31905.

Schneitter, E. (2016). States and prescription drugs: An overview of state programs to rein in costs. National Academy for State Health Care Policy. https://nashp.org/wp-content/uploads/2016/04/Drug-Brief.pdf

Schoenbrod, D., R. B. Stewart, and K. M. Wyman. (2012). *Breaking the Logjam: Environmental Protection That Will Work*. New Haven, CT: Yale University Press.

Schor, E. (2010). Socially responsible investors push TSCA reform. *Greenwire*, September 27 (online).

Service, R. F. (2009). A new wave of chemical regulations just ahead? *Science*, 325(5941): 692–693.

Silbergeld, E. K., D. Mandrioli, and C. F. Cranor. (2015). Regulating chemicals: Law, science, and the unbearable burdens of regulation. *Annual Review of Public Health*, 36: 175–191.

Silver, N. (2016). Donald Trump has a 20 percent chance of becoming president, June 29. https://fivethirtyeight.com/features/donald-trump-has-a-20-percent-chance-of-becoming-president/

Smith, S. S., J. M. Roberts, and R. J. Vander Wielen. (2015). *The American Congress*, 9th edn, New York: Cambridge University Press.

Stephenson, J. M. (2006). *Testimony, Committee on Environmental and Chemical Regulation: Actions Are Needed to Improve the Effectiveness of EPA's Chemical Review Program*. Washington, DC: U.S. Senate Committee on Environmental and Public Works.

Stigler, G. J. (1971). The theory of regulation. *Bell Journal of Economics and Management Science*, 2(1): 3–21.

Szal, A. (2016). Will the EPA be up to the task of enforcing TSCA reform rules? *Chem.info*, June 8 (online).

Tausanovitch, C., and C. Warshaw. (2016). Estimating candidate positions in a polarized Congress. Working paper, Massachusetts Institute of Technology.

Teter, M. J. (2013). Congressional gridlock's threat to separation of powers. *Wisconsin Law Review*, 2013(6): 1097–1160.

Tollefson, J. (2016). US chemicals law set for overhaul: Bill would give government more authority to regulate potentially toxic substances. *Nature*, 534(7605): 18–19. June 2.

The Toxic Substances Control Act: From the Perspective of Charles M. Auer. (2010). Interview by Jody A. Roberts and Kavita D. Hardy in Washington, DC. Apr. 23. Philadelphia: Chemical Heritage Foundation, Oral History Transcript.

The Toxic Substances Control Act: From the Perspective of Don R. Clay. (2010). Interview by Jody A. Roberts and Kavita D. Hardy at Koch Industries, Inc., Washington, DC, March 16. Philadelphia: Chemical Heritage Foundation, Oral History Transcript.

The Toxic Substances Control Act: From the Perspective of Glenn E. Schweitzer. (2010). Interview by Jody A. Roberts at the National Academy of Sciences, Washington, DC, Dec. 29. Philadelphia: Chemical Heritage Foundation, Oral History Transcript.

The Toxic Substances Control Act: From the Perspective of J. Clarence Davies. (2010). Interview by Jody A. Roberts and Kavita D. Hardy in Washington, DC. Oct. 30, 2009. Philadelphia: Chemical Heritage Foundation, Oral History Transcript.

The Toxic Substances Control Act: From the Perspective of James V. Aidala. (2010). Interview by Jody A. Roberts and Kavita D. Hardy at Bergeson & Campbell P. C. Washington, DC, May 20. Philadelphia: Chemical Heritage Foundation, Oral History Transcript.

The Toxic Substances Control Act: From the Perspective of Steven D. Jellinek. (2010). Interview by Jody A. Roberts and Kavita D. Hardy at The Chemical Heritage Foundation, Philadelphia, Pennsylvania, Jan. 29. Philadelphia: Chemical Heritage Foundation, Oral History Transcript.

The Toxic Substances Control Act: From the Perspective of Victor J. Kimm. (2011). Interview by Jody A. Roberts at Ropes & Gray LLP.,

Washington, DC, Feb. 3. Philadelphia: Chemical Heritage Foundation, Oral History Transcript.

Tullo, A. H. (2016). C&EN's global top 50. *Chemical & Engineering News* 94 (30): 32–37.

U.S. Government Accountability Office. (2007). Chemical regulation: Comparison of U.S. and recently enacted European Union approaches to protect against the risks of toxic chemicals. GAO Report GAO-07-825.

U.S. Government Accounting Office. (1994). Toxic Substances Control Act: Legislative changes could make the Act more effective. GAO Report RCED-94-103.

U.S. House, Committee on Energy and Commerce. (2009). *Revisiting the Toxic Substances Control Act of 1976*, Washington, DC: US Government Printing Office.

U.S. House, Committee on Interstate and Foreign Commerce. (1976). *Legislative History of the Toxic Substances Control Act*, Washington, DC: US Government Printing Office.

U.S. Senate, Committee on Energy and Public Works. (1994). *Reauthorization of the Toxic Substances Control Act*, Washington, DC: U.S. Government Printing Office.

Van Norman, G. S. (2016). Drug and devices: Comparison of U.S. and European approval processes. *JACC: Basic to Translational Science* 1 (5): 399–412.

Vaughn, S. (2015). *EU Chemicals Regulation: New Governance, Hybridity and Reach*. Cheltenham: Edward Elgar.

Vogel, S. A., and J. A. Roberts. (2011). Why the Toxic Substances Control Act needs an overhaul, and how to strengthen oversight of chemicals in the interim. *Health Affairs*, 30(5): 898–905.

Walsh, E. (2017). EPA's asbestos evaluation shows strong support for and against a ban. *The MCA Blog*, www.mesothelioma.com/blog/authors/emily/epas-asbestos-evaluation-shows-strong-support-for-and-against-a-ban.htm.

Walsh, W. J., and M. M. Skjoldal. (2011). Sustainability is driving toxic chemicals from products. *Natural Resources & Environment*, 25(3): 16–20.

Welsh, H., and M. Passoff. (2016). *Proxy Preview 2016*. Oakland, CA: As You Sow.

Wilson, M. P., and M. R. Schwarzman. (2011). Science, green chemistry, and environmental health. In H. H. Trimm and W Hunter III, eds., *Industrial Chemistry: New Applications, Processes and Systems*, Boca Raton, FL: CRC Press, pp. 176–201.

Winder, C., R. Azzi, and D. Wagner. (2005). The development of the globally harmonized system (GHS) of classification and labelling of hazardous chemicals. *Journal of Hazardous Materials*, 125(1–3): 29–44.

Yohannan, S. (2016). Shimkus says TSCA reform creates model to fix "broker" Superfund law. *Inside EPA*, 37(28) (online).

Printed in the United States
By Bookmasters